THE UNIVERSITY OF ALABAMA

THE UNIVERSITY OF ALABAMA
A Guide to the Campus and Its Architecture

ROBERT OLIVER MELLOWN

The University of Alabama Press • Tuscaloosa

Copyright © 2013
The University of Alabama Press
Tuscaloosa, Alabama 35487-0380
All rights reserved
Manufactured in the United States of America

Typeface: Garamond Premiere Pro

Cover photograph: Clark Hall. Courtesy of Duane A. Lamb.
Frontispiece: Denny Chimes
Design: Michele Myatt Quinn

∞

The paper on which this book is printed meets the minimum
requirements of American National Standard for Information
Sciences—Permanence of Paper for Printed Library Materials,
ANSI Z39.48-1984.

Library of Congress Cataloging-in-Publication Data

Mellown, Robert O.
The University of Alabama : a guide to the campus and its architecture / Robert Oliver Mellown.
     pages   cm
Includes index.
ISBN 978-0-8173-5680-4 (quality paper : alk. paper)—ISBN
978-0-8173-8673-3 (ebook) 1. University of Alabama—Buildings—Guidebooks. 2. Tuscaloosa (Ala.)—Buildings, structures,
etc.—Guidebooks. I. Title.
LD74.M45 2013
378.761'84—dc23   2012050729

To the memory of Richard Henry Mellown (1945–2011)

Contents

Preface   ix

Acknowledgments   xi

How to Use This Guide   xiii

An Architectural History of the University of Alabama   1

1 Antebellum Campus Tour   36

2 Victorian Campus Tour   62

3 Early Twentieth-Century Campus Tour   78

4 East Quad Tour   88

5 West Quad Tour   102

6 Science and Engineering Corridor Tour   120

7 Student Life Campus Tour   136

8 Bryce Campus Tour   148

9 Medical Campus Tour   158

10 Southeast Campus Tour   166

11 Athletics Campus Tour   174

12 Off Campus Tours   184

Glossary   195

Suggested Reading   201

Photograph Credits   203

Index   205

Preface

I grew to love the Victorian buildings surrounding the Old Quadrangle at the University of Alabama as an undergraduate art student
in the 1960s. Later in 1971, after four years of graduate study at the
University of North Carolina at Chapel Hill, I returned to the Capstone as a freshly minted art historian. For forty years I frequently
used campus buildings in my lectures to illustrate architectural styles
and as examples of good (and bad) design and planning. Over time
I came to realize that these structures also revealed much about the
aspirations of Alabamians, their values, and their attitudes concerning
higher education. In 1988 at the suggestion of Malcolm MacDonald,
director of the University of Alabama Press, I wrote *The University of
Alabama: A Guide to the Campus* in which I examined the Capstone's
architectural history through a series of tours. Since writing that book
many changes have transformed the face of the university. In 2009
Dr. Lynda Gilbert, vice president for Financial Affairs and treasurer
for the University of Alabama, urged me to create a new version of
the guide that would reflect the greatly expanded twenty-first-century
campus of this venerable institution.

The University of Alabama campus began as a small group of
buildings located near the outskirts of the village of Tuscaloosa.
Today over 180 years later it consists of about 300 buildings located
on approximately 2,000 acres of land surrounded by a constantly
growing city. Nevertheless, the campus remains "a place apart" with
its own distinct characteristics, traditions, and legends. The purpose
of this guide is to acquaint members of the university community and
visitors with the rich heritage of this institution through a study of
select buildings, monuments, and sites.

Acknowledgments

A number of people have helped to make possible this new revised and expanded guide. My thanks to Dr. Lynda Gilbert, vice president for Financial Affairs and treasurer for the University of Alabama, for suggesting this project and for the financial support of the university administration. I have benefitted from her suggestions and those of Tim Leopard, assistant vice president for Construction Administration; Duane Lamb, assistant vice president for Facilities and Grounds Operations; and Dan Wolfe, university planner and designer. Carolyn Hyde, Plan Room coordinator, Construction Administration, was also most helpful in identifying architects and contractors of the newer campus buildings and tracking down architectural renderings of them. Craig Remington, director of the university's Cartography Laboratory, created maps specifically for this guide.

The handsome images illustrating this book were taken by a number of photographers. Many were provided by the staff of Cathy Andreen, director of Media Relations at the University of Alabama. Duane Lamb, mentioned above, allowed us to use many of his personal photographs of university sites and structures. I owe a special debt to Rachel Dobson, visual resources curator in the Department of Art and Art History, who not only produced a number of the digital images used in this guide, but also assisted me in many ways including the selection and organization of the scores of photographs taken during this project. I also gratefully acknowledge the use of archival images from the William Stanley Hoole Special Collections Library including Teresa Golson's photograph of the library's Tiffany window. Clark Center, retired university archivist and curator for the Southern History and Life Collection, and Jessica Lacher-Feldman, curator of Rare Books and Special Collections, were particularly helpful.

My thanks to the former University of Alabama Press director Dan Ross and to editor-in-chief Dan Waterman for their many helpful suggestions, and for bearing with me as I struggled to shape this material into a coherent and readable guide. I am also most grateful for the assistance of Crissie Johnson, managing editor of the University of Alabama Press and project editor for this book, and for copyeditor Dawn Hall's careful editing of the text.

I also acknowledge the assistance of my friend and former colleague Dr. James McNutt and of my brother Dr. Elgin Mellown Jr., who read early versions of the manuscript and made many helpful suggestions.

How to Use This Guide

This guide begins with an essay on the history of the development and planning of the campus from the establishment of the university in 1820 up to the present day. It is followed by a series of on-campus tours as well as one of off-campus sites associated with the university. Stops on the tours consist of selected buildings, sites, and monuments that are keyed to a general campus map located in the front and end papers of the guide and to specific maps located at the beginning of each tour.

It is suggested that visitors park in designated areas in the Ferguson Center Parking Deck [A], North ten Hoor Parking Deck [B], or the Campus Drive Parking Deck [C]. Parking passes are also available for purchase at the Transportation Services office located in the Student Services Center [66]. These facilities are within walking distance of buildings and sites discussed in the first six tours in this guide. The last five are designed primarily as windshield tours.

Since many visitors to the university do not have the time to indulge in a leisurely investigation of the campus in its entirety, this guide may be used topographically. If pressed for time, make up your own tour by consulting the maps or the Building Index and turn to the appropriate sections in the text.

For footsore tourists the wheelchair-accessible campus bus system is an excellent (and free) alternative to walking about this large campus. Buses are clearly marked, and with a little advance planning and two or three changes, one is able to view all of the campus sights mentioned in the guide without the ordeal of dealing with traffic. Do not worry about getting lost—the bus routes are circular, so you will eventually get back to where you started.

The guide is also designed for armchair observers. Depending on your location (or inclination), put on a comfortable pair of walking shoes and proceed to the Rotunda [1], or take *off* your shoes and curl up in a comfortable chair and get ready to explore the complex, sometimes violent (but always fascinating) history of the campus of the state's oldest institution of higher learning, the University of Alabama.

THE UNIVERSITY OF ALABAMA

An Architectural History of the University of Alabama

The University of Alabama was officially established by an act of the state legislature on December 18, 1820, but its history actually began two years earlier when the US Congress set aside an entire township in the Alabama Territory for the support of a "seminary of learning." Congress granted a second township for the school's support upon Alabama's entrance into the Union in 1819. These lands, totaling 46,080 acres, were to be rented, leased, or sold to create "a fund for the exclusive support of a state University." For almost a decade, however, the University of Alabama was only an abstract legal entity existing on paper, its assets managed by a board of trustees.

The Antebellum Campus, 1828–65

In 1827 the board of trustees determined that sufficient funds had been raised to construct a campus. To avoid sectional disputes, they decided to place it as near the center of the state as was possible. After thirteen locations were considered and nineteen ballots cast, Tuscaloosa, a town only recently designated the state capital, was chosen as the site for the campus of the University of Alabama. The trustees then determined to build the school on part of an original land grant known as Marr's Field, a tract once farmed by William M. Marr and located about a mile and a half east of the Tuscaloosa County Courthouse. Fifty adjacent acres were purchased to keep "immoral persons" from settling on them, and also to take advantage of the nearby timber and the clay deposits that were needed for construction of the buildings.

The campus was designed according to the plans provided by the state architect, William Nichols, who was then living in Tuscaloosa and supervising the construction of an impressive new capitol. Like the statehouse, Nichols designed the campus in the Classical Revival style inspired by ancient Greek and Roman architecture. This style, with its origins in the eighteenth-century Enlightenment, relied heavily for inspiration upon books such as Andrea Palladio's *Quattro*

Libre, first published in 1570, and James Stuart and Nicholas Revett's *Antiquities of Athens,* published between 1762 and 1816. Over the years a consensus among educated gentlemen, builders, and architects developed as to what constituted appropriate combinations and borrowings from Greek, Roman, and even Egyptian architecture for the construction of modern buildings. By the time Nichols designed the capitol and university in Tuscaloosa, classical references in architecture were commonly used as visual metaphors to communicate such abstract concepts as Greek "culture" and Roman "gravitas," and also to proclaim the young Republic's values and convictions. Such ideas were very much on the minds of the members of the board of trustees who, as early as 1822, had adopted a handsome official seal. Governor Israel Pickens requested the Philadelphia company that made it to include on its circumscription the abbreviated Latin phrase *Universitat. Alabam. Sigil.,* and that the design should "significantly represent the *light of science beaming on this hemisphere* so lately emerged from a heathenish wilderness." The seal depicted Athena, goddess of wisdom, a nimbus of light radiating about her head, pointing with a compass in her right hand to a globe. In her left hand she points with an olive branch (a symbol of her gift to the Athenians) to the Acropolis in the background on which they had built her cult temple, the Parthenon. A version of the great seal is still in use today and has been used to ornament a number of buildings on campus. However, its imagery over

the years has been sadly debased. It has lost its Latin circumscription and its symbolism has been rendered meaningless, Athena's nimbus being misinterpreted as a rising sun and the Parthenon being replaced by a cotton plant!

William Nichols was an Englishman, born in Bath and educated there. He arrived in the United States about 1800 and first constructed buildings in New Bern, Edenton, and Fayetteville, North Carolina. In 1818 he was appointed North Carolina's architect and was made responsible for the remodeling of the capitol and governor's mansion in Raleigh. In addition, Nichols designed several buildings and remodeled others at the University of North Carolina at Chapel Hill. In 1827 he resigned that post to become state architect and engineer of Alabama. His most important architectural commissions were both in Tuscaloosa: the design and construction of the state capitol (1827; burned 1923) and the University of Alabama campus (1828; burned 1865), but his Alabama production also included the earliest work on the Muscle Shoals Canal and a survey for the state's first railroad. After leaving Alabama in 1833, Nichols went to Louisiana and, as state engineer, finished the penitentiary in Baton Rouge and remodeled the statehouse in New Orleans. In 1836 he was appointed state architect of Mississippi. There, a number of his buildings still survive, including the old capitol and governor's mansion in Jackson, and the Lyceum at the University of Mississippi.

FIGURE 2 The University of Alabama Seal designed in 1822 by Murray Draper Fairman & Co. in Philadelphia at the request of Governor Israel Pickens, ex officio president of the board of trustees of the University of Alabama.

Author's rendering.

Nichols's design for the Alabama capitol was derived from his plans for the remodeling of the North Carolina statehouse. His plan for the University of Alabama campus was based in part on his previous work at the University of North Carolina. At that institution the principal classroom building headed a grand avenue that was flanked on each side by student dormitories. Nichols used this idea at Alabama in the placement of the main academic building (the Laboratory, later called the Lyceum) and in the arrangement of the two rows of dormitories. However, he grafted onto the North Carolina plan (for which he was partly responsible) certain ideas that he borrowed from Thomas Jefferson's University of Virginia at Charlottesville.

Long before Nichols had arrived in Alabama the University Board of Trustees had become interested in the construction of the Virginia campus. On June 13, 1822, Governor Pickens wrote President Jefferson at Monticello that he was "desirous to procure for the use of the board the plan of building adopted for the University of Virginia which has been favoured by your patronage; and also the system of government & instruction. . . . In procuring which any assistance you may have the kindness to render will be thankfully appreciated; and the more especially if accompanied with your own views on such points as you may deem useful to this infant institution." Jefferson's reply to this request (if he made one) has not been located. Nevertheless, the construction of the Virginia campus obviously continued to interest the Alabama board of trustees whose records four and a half years later recounted that a Mr. Beene had presented it with "a ground plan of the University of Virginia."

Like Jefferson's design, Nichols's campus plan provided for a complete collegiate town, or "academical village," to be located at some distance in the country to reduce the temptations and distractions of town. Buildings for classrooms and for housing students and faculty members and their families were arranged around the sides of a parklike green or common. In each plan the library, a rotunda, was made the center of interest of the ensemble. The idea of having faculty members and their families live on campus with classrooms located in their homes, or contiguous to them, was an unusual feature of both designs. Paul Venable Turner pointed out in his 1988 *Campus: An American Building Tradition* that this element in Jefferson's Virginia campus was "too demanding and inflexible for most American institutions, and was almost never adopted elsewhere." William Nichols, however, used the idea not only at the University of Alabama but again at the University of Mississippi in Oxford.

Nichols's ambitious Alabama plan called for a two-story, temple-fronted building, the Laboratory or Lyceum, on the northern end of campus, flanked on either side by three-story faculty duplexes. These were connected by one-story recitation rooms. Four large "colleges," or dormitories for students, and two steward's halls containing dining rooms were located on the east and west sides of the campus. The focal point of the ensemble was the Rotunda, containing a library and commencement hall. The south side of campus was eventually to be closed with buildings similar to those on the north end, and these were to house the proposed medical school.

Although the University of Alabama was planned and built as an institution of higher learning with a residential campus, in 1860, largely due to the influence of President Landon Cabell Garland, the board of trustees inaugurated a military form of governance destined to continue for the next forty-three years. The change proved to be a popular one, even with civilian professors, who believed that a regimented student life would solve the problems of discipline that had

FIGURE 4 The Rotunda viewed from the roof of the President's Mansion, ca. 1859. The only known photograph of the antebellum university. From Dominique Doux Fiquet's "Album of Friendship, 1859."

Courtesy of the W. S. Hoole Special Collections Library, the University of Alabama.

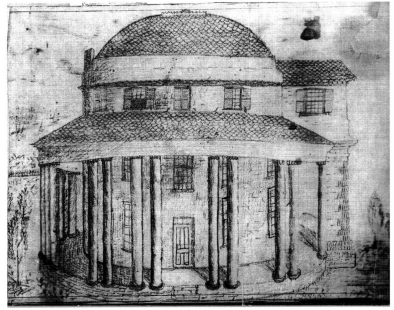

FIGURE 5 Drawing of the west side of the Rotunda by university student John Henry Glascock, 1864.

Courtesy of the W. S. Hoole Special Collections Library, the University of Alabama.

plagued the institution for years. It cannot be doubted, however, that another reason was the ever-present talk of secession and probable war with the North—and young Alabamians wanted to be prepared. Indeed, when war was declared, the faculty found it increasingly difficult to retain the students for the full program. Many, after receiving only the rudiments of military training, left the university to join the Confederate forces.

UNIVERSITY OF ALABAMA, TUSCALOOSA.

Despite the change of governance, the campus remained relatively unchanged and bore a close resemblance to the original design before Federal troops almost completely destroyed it at the close of the Civil War.

THE VICTORIAN CAMPUS, 1865–1906

Plans to reopen the devastated university began almost immediately after the Federal raid of April 4, 1865. The President's Mansion [4], the largest of the remaining campus buildings, was to be used for classrooms and dormitories until other arrangements could be made, but since only one student showed up for classes on October 1, 1865, when the university was scheduled to reopen, this plan was never put into effect. Two months later the board of trustees voted to rebuild the campus rather than attempt to reopen the institution in the surviving buildings. The legislature provided funds, and within a week a building committee began work with President Garland. This com-

FIGURE 6 University letterhead depicting the entrance to the cedar-lined avenue leading to the Rotunda. Woodcut ca. 1861.

Courtesy of the W. S. Hoole Special Collections Library, the University of Alabama.

mittee reviewed about eighteen plans for college campuses. In the meantime, however, because the trustees had determined to retain the military system in effect since 1860, only those plans suitable for a military school were considered, and plans for civilian colleges were returned to their architects.

The building committee finally settled on the design Alexander Jackson Davis of New York had submitted. His plan had been drawn earlier, actually in the 1840s, for the construction of Virginia Military Institute (VMI) in Lexington. Davis was one of the most influential and prolific of nineteenth-century American architects. Although his reputation must have played a part in the selection process, it was probably not the key factor, for the committee was very likely influenced by several members of the university faculty who were prewar graduates of VMI and had studied in Davis's buildings.

Davis had designed his VMI campus in the English Gothic or Tudor style, which he, more than any other architect, helped to foster in the 1830s and 1840s. The main building in his design, the barracks, consisted of a large four-story rectangle facing inward toward an enclosed courtyard. Rooms—none of which connected on the upper

FIGURE 8 Ruins of the Lyceum, by an unknown artist, 1866. The foundations of this structure lie under Clark Hall. Several of the sandstone Ionic capitals from the Lyceum and the nearby Rotunda are now displayed in the Hoole Special Collections Library.

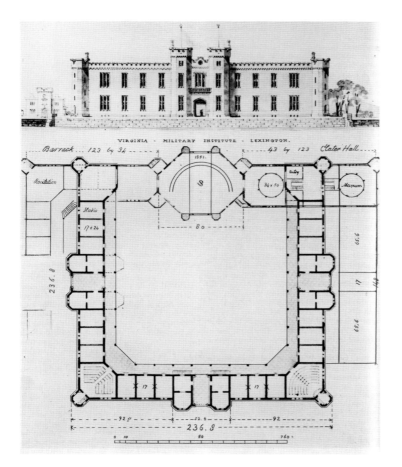

FIGURE 9 Plan and Elevation of the Virginia Military Institute, Lexington, Virginia. A. J. Davis, architect.

floors—opened onto porches, or "piazzas." The benefits of such a plan for a military school were based upon rigid rules and discipline. Once in their quarters, cadets could not leave without being observed. Furthermore, if the doors or gates to the inner courtyard were secured, it was impossible to leave the building undetected. The overall effect of the main building was highly picturesque, with its hundreds of feet of battlements, narrow hood-molded windows, buttresses, and polygonal towers.

Before returning the plans to Davis, the building committee made a copy of them and modified them to reflect the suggestions made by Captain John F. Gibbs who, before coming to Alabama, had served twelve years at VMI.

The building committee selected the commandant of cadets, Colonel James T. Murfee, as architect for the proposed new structure. Murfee was a natural choice. Not only was he a graduate of VMI with a knowledge of the advantages and disadvantages of the Davis plan, but he was also a builder with the construction of one school already to his credit. During his four years at the Virginia institution (he graduated first in his class in 1853) he had witnessed the completion of Davis's buildings. In 1856, while teaching mathematics and natural science at Lynchburg College in Lynchburg, Virginia, Murfee had been given the job of designing that school's building.

Colonel Murfee determined to place the new building at the University of Alabama behind the ruins of the Lyceum, on the northern edge of campus and facing the President's Mansion [4] to the south. His intention was to transform the site of the prewar campus into a large and completely fenced park that would secure it from the damages of wandering livestock. It would be, he said, a place where "students, officers, ladies, gentlemen, and children may meet, as in the parks of a city, for social conversation, mental and physical recreation." This "park" with its ruins, now known as the Main Quadrangle, or simply the Quad, was an area that elicited strong feelings. For many Alabamians it was sacred ground, and they responded to it in much the same way the ancient Athenians had done to their ruined acropolis, destroyed by the Persian Invasion of 480 BC. (Rather than rebuild, the Athenians had originally intended to leave the destroyed buildings as war memorials and a constant reminder to remain vigilant.) At the University of Alabama a decade after the Federal incursion a writer for the April 29, 1875, *Tuscaloosa Blade* suggested

FIGURE 10 The Barracks (later named Woods Hall), based on the VMI plan and built in 1868, was the first building to be erected on campus after the Civil War. Eugene Allen Smith photograph, ca. 1890.

Courtesy of the W. S. Hoole Special Collections Library, the University of Alabama.

that the campus ruins be left as a reminder for future generations of the senseless destruction of war and the "nation's folly" for resorting to it to solve its internal disputes.

The proposed new edifice based on the VMI plan was so large that only one-half, Woods Hall, was initially built in 1867–68. That portion was used for fifteen years for all university functions. After supervising the construction of the university building, Murfee left Tuscaloosa for Marion, Alabama, where he served as president of Howard College (now Samford University). He remained in Marion when that school moved to Birmingham in 1887, acquired the school's former campus, and established Marion Military Institute.

In the prosperous 1880s, the University of Alabama's financial situation improved to the extent that it was possible to contemplate further additions to the campus. As early as 1881 the board of trustees formed a committee to work in concert with the alumni to secure funds for enlarging the barracks and for constructing a chapel for public exercises. The following year Senator John Tyler Morgan was successful in securing funds from Congress to recompense the University of Alabama for the destruction of the campus during the Civil War. A year later the trustees established another building committee with authority to review and evaluate plans for the new buildings. After reviewing the plans of several architects the committee selected those of William Alfred Freret, of New Orleans.

Freret was probably the foremost architect of Louisiana. The son

of William Freret, a former mayor of New Orleans, he had studied
engineering and architecture in France before the Civil War. His large
family had close ties with Mobile, and it is possible that Willis G.
Clark, a native of that city and an influential member of the board,
was instrumental in his appointment. In 1880 Freret had received the
commission to restore the Louisiana capitol in Baton Rouge, another
structure burned during the Civil War.

Freret's most recent commissions had been the design and construction of a series of ornate Victorian public schools and the
Touro-Shakespeare Almshouse in New Orleans.

Freret must have persuaded the trustees that Colonel Murfee's
original plan for the enlargement of Woods Hall was old-fashioned. It
probably did not take much to convince them. Despite its highly practical and functional design, the barracks was not ideal for a university
building. Rather than imitate the VMI model, now almost forty years
old, Freret adapted it to meet the needs of the present and to reflect
current architectural tastes. Today we refer to this style as High Vic-

torian Gothic, but at the time "the general style of the buildings" was described as "ecclesiastical Gothic, modified so as to harmonize with the Tudor style of the present building [Woods Hall]." Rather than create another massive building similar to and joining the barracks, he proposed to build three independent structures: a central building (now Clark Hall [12] and two wings, now Manly [13] and Garland [14] halls). These wings were designed so that they could be enlarged and connected to Woods Hall as additional space became necessary. Because of the expense only Clark and Manly halls were erected in 1884 and plans to connect all four buildings were, perhaps fortunately, never carried out. After completing the University of Alabama commission Freret enjoyed a prosperous career, and he was appointed supervising architect of the US Treasury. As such he was put in charge of designing federal buildings and US courthouses across the country.

FIGURE 12 Barnard and Tuomey halls in the foreground of this print were the last buildings to be erected on the campus in the nineteenth century. "Bird's Eye View, Alabama State University." Woodcut by Henderson-Achert, Cincinnati, Ohio, engraver, from Willis G. Clark, *History of Education in Alabama 1702–1889* (Washington, DC: Government Printing Office, 1889).

THE GREATER UNIVERSITY PLAN, 1906

The first decade of the twentieth century brought many changes to the University of Alabama. First, and perhaps most significant, President John W. Abercrombie abolished the military form of governance and replaced it with a system of schools and colleges on which the present institution is still based. To put the university on a more competitive level with comparable institutions in neighboring states, Abercrombie worked tirelessly to raise academic standards. New classrooms and other physical facilities for adequate instruction, new students, and a stronger faculty were mandatory. Working with the Society of the Alumni, Abercrombie launched a campaign to raise money for new buildings. The present appearance of the central campus owes much to the results of this successful fund drive, geared to coincide with the university's seventy-fifth anniversary in 1906.

THE GREATER UNIVERSITY CAMPAIGN

In 1905, the Society of the Alumni had gathered to plan for a much-needed new geological museum. But a far more ambitious project—a total planning program for the university—emerged. The resulting Greater University Committee met again in January 1906 and determined that there was an immediate need not only for a museum but also for an academic building, a gymnasium, a library, and a larger endowment from the legislature to support the university and its programs. Before the meeting was over the committee had ratified a plan. According to an article in the May 30, 1906, *Montgomery Advertiser:* "There is to be no haphazard architecture, no patch work construction with a building of this sort one year and a building of that sort another year. The plan is comprehensive and it looks forward a full century. This particular building on the plan may not be constructed for twenty-five years, but its special place on the plan has been selected and set aside and today it is known what the style and architecture is to be." Moreover, members raised $500 for engaging the "best experts" in the country to come and review the needs of the campus and make recommendations.

Hill Ferguson and Robert Jemison were instrumental in the selection of the professionals the committee chose. These two Birmingham businessmen were currently developing Mountain Terrace, a subdivision in the "Magic City," with the well-known New York architectural firm Samuel Parsons and Company in charge. Ferguson suggested that the Society of the Alumni also employ this firm as consultants.

Parsons and Company specialized in landscape architecture. Its founder, Samuel Parsons Jr., had been a partner of architect Calvert Vaux in the 1880s when Parsons was appointed superintendent of planting in Central Park. Eventually, he became landscape architect and commissioner of parks for the city of New York. In addition, his

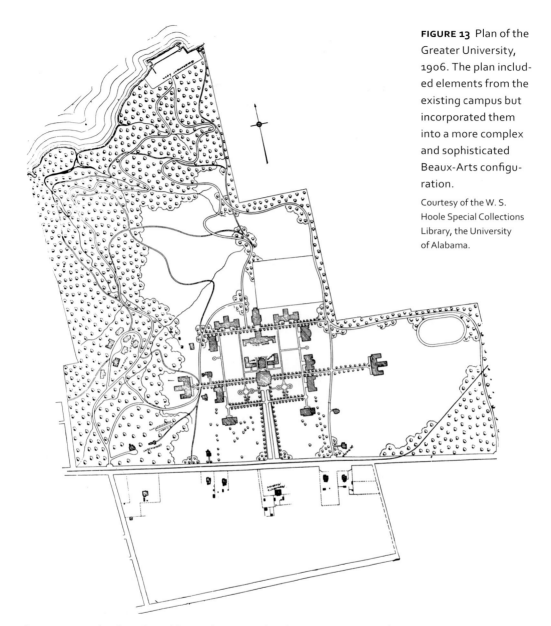

FIGURE 13 Plan of the Greater University, 1906. The plan included elements from the existing campus but incorporated them into a more complex and sophisticated Beaux-Arts configuration.

Courtesy of the W. S. Hoole Special Collections Library, the University of Alabama.

firm was involved with public and private development in a number of states.

The actual planning for the revitalization of the university was done by George Cooke, a member of the firm, who immediately recommended that the area from the rear of Woods Hall to the Black Warrior River be developed as a park with winding drives ornamented with memorial iron gates bearing the dates of graduating classes. Although it took a century to bring it about, a variation of this idea of a

park was accomplished in the first decade of the twenty-first century (see the Park at Manderson's Landing [104]).

Cooke was particularly concerned about the lack of attention given to the many old trees on campus. He requested that all the mature trees be identified on a special contour map being prepared by Professor Edgar B. Kay, dean of the School of Engineering, and that many of them be utilized in the projected campus plan.

The scheme for the Greater University Campus was very much a product of the Beaux-Arts architectural planning developed at the École des Beaux-Arts, the official French art school in Paris. Introduced to the American public at the 1893 World's Columbian Exposition in Chicago, this system consisted of symmetry, axiality, focal points, and geometric clarity, all of which were found to be readily adaptable to urban planning and particularly to American universities

and colleges. Over the last century these had ceased to be "academical villages" of several buildings, as conceived by Jefferson and Nichols, and had become, in effect, "academical cities" composed of many complex structures, with uses of which earlier planners had never dreamed. This new French planning system allowed modern designers to give such large, heterogeneous campuses a visual and functional unity.

To achieve this unity architects preferred to design campuses from the ground up. Frequently, however, as at the University of Alabama, they were faced with the problem of what to do with old buildings having considerable sentimental value to the alumni. The problem was particularly acute at the university, where a military system had only recently been abandoned, and the campus still included barracks and a parade ground. To make matters worse, the old buildings were

FIGURE 14 Rendering of the proposed Greater University, 1906. Hughson Hawley, illustrator. Created for promotional purposes, the illustration provided alumni and prospective donors with a vision of how the campus might be developed in the twentieth century. Courtesy of the W. S. Hoole Special Collections Library, the University of Alabama.

designed in the now despised Gothic Revival and High Victorian Gothic styles. Not surprisingly, in his rendering of the new campus, Parsons designer Hughson Hawley—the foremost architectural illustrator of the era—would have preferred to ignore these buildings. The intention was clear: the old campus should be demolished as soon as newer buildings were constructed to take their places. Governor Braxton Bragg Comer, an Alabama alumnus whose school days had been spent in the buildings of the old antebellum campus, subscribed to this view. In a speech to the legislature in 1906 he stated: "The University, once the pride of the State, was burned in 1865 by supposed military necessity. Rebuilt, it is true, but that rebuilding was like the restoration of the temple and walls of Jerusalem by Nehemiah, Ezra, and Zerubbabel; when the work was completed and compared with the old Jerusalem, they sat themselves down and wept."

Hill Ferguson, a much younger alumnus whose school days had been spent in the buildings of the postwar campus, however, insisted that the Victorian structures be included at least temporarily in the master plan and in the rendering. He realized that more recent alumni would never accept a scheme that entirely wiped out their familiar alma mater. Cooke reluctantly agreed to instruct his draftsmen and artist to include the old buildings, and they did so—but without enthusiasm. Ferguson also requested that the plan include the campus "mounds," but the designers responded by leveling them and marking their locations with geometrically patterned flower beds. Ferguson ordered that the Gorgas House [8], Student Fortifications [6], Observatory [5], President's Mansion [4], and various faculty houses also be salvaged from the old nineteenth-century campus.

Many members of the Society of the Alumni had vivid memories of the Neoclassical, antebellum campus, and they looked back on their school days with great nostalgia. It is therefore not unusual that Cooke and his artists turned to an engraving of the old university campus for inspiration (see fig. 1) in placing and forming the new campus buildings. Indeed, the Greater University Plan was nothing less than William Nichols's design reinterpreted through the eyes of a Beaux-Arts-trained architect, enlarged to a much grander scale, and adapted to meet the demands of a modern university. Even the domed central building was to be on the site of the original Rotunda.

The color of the proposed buildings recalled the antebellum campus as well. Yellow brick was a highly popular building material in the first two decades of the twentieth century, but its use for the new campus may possibly have been suggested by some of the older alumni who recalled their school days in the old buildings. In 1851, President Basil Manly had ordered that the Lyceum, Rotunda, and dormitories be painted a yellowish-tan. Living alumni would probably have remembered their alma mater thus.

Following current architectural fashion, the Greater University buildings were to be Classical Revival in style, with specific details to be worked out later. Eager to get the plan and the architectural rendering as soon as possible, Hill Ferguson suggested to Cooke that they use recently constructed New York academic buildings for inspiration. It was not even necessary to specify the uses of the illustrated buildings at this point. The main objective was to be able to present this glorious vision of the university's future campus during the seventy-fifth anniversary celebration in May 1906.

The success of the campaign hinged upon winning the support of the incumbent governor, Braxton Bragg Comer. Initially skeptical of the scope of the plan, Comer was won over by the arguments of President Abercrombie and Ferguson. Ferguson later recalled that they had persuaded Comer to "give liberal support to the higher institution of learning in order to provide teachers for his proposed high school program, which was one of his favored projects."

The committee sent colored prints of the architectural rendering of the Greater University Campus (see fig. 14) and other promotional literature to the incoming legislature and to friends and alumni throughout the state. In addition, alumni banquets were held in Birmingham, Mobile, Montgomery, and other cities to generate interest in the campaign, and these efforts proved highly successful. In 1907 the legislature passed an "act to Provide for the Better Equipment and Support of the University of Alabama, and to Appropriate Funds therefore." Not only did it provide funds, but it also specified and ranked the first four buildings to be erected. Significantly, it did not include a gymnasium, a top priority with the alumni. The legislature apparently supported President Abercrombie, who was determined to de-emphasize athletics. The first building to be constructed was to house the biology and geology departments as well as the natural history museum (Smith Hall [20]); the second was to contain civil, mining, electrical, and mechanical engineering (Comer Hall [18]); the third was designated the "academic building" (Morgan Hall [19]);

and the fourth was to be a much-needed women's dormitory (Tut-wiler Hall [22]).

The man hired to design the buildings, renovate the older structures, and carry out other aspects of the Greater University Plan was Montgomery architect Frank Lockwood. Like William Nichols, who had designed the original campus in 1828 after designing the Alabama capitol in Tuscaloosa, Lockwood had only recently (1905) completed construction of the north and south wings of the state capitol in Montgomery. Although he was born in Trenton, New Jersey, in 1865, his family's background—like Nichols's—was English. His father, a mechanical engineer, had come to the United States to superintend the construction of the Brooklyn Bridge. The younger Lockwood had studied in New York under the well-known architect George B. Post. It was while he was working with Post that Lockwood was sent to Anniston, Alabama, on a commission. Later, after working for two years in Columbus, Georgia, he had moved to Montgomery where he was responsible not only for enlarging the state capitol but also for designing numerous secondary schools and colleges throughout the state.

Lockwood did not follow the university's proposed master plan in every detail, and the layout of the campus, as built, was actually considerably different from the original drawings. Nevertheless, for good or ill, the Greater University Plan set the precedent for a campus in the Classical Revival style with buildings located in formal, Beaux-Arts configurations. This design was followed for the next sixty-five years.

The Million Dollar Plan, 1925

When George H. Denny became president of the University of Alabama in 1912, 652 students were enrolled. When he retired twenty-five years later, there were more than five thousand. Despite this steady increase in students, funds for enlarging the campus had not been forthcoming from the legislature. By 1920 the need for additional space was critical. Denny declared that fifteen buildings were immediately necessary, and he estimated that "a million dollars" was needed to construct them. Two years later, the Society of the Alumni, backed by the board of trustees, used Denny's cost estimate as the theme of their "Million Dollar Campaign." The design and construction of the Quadrangle and the buildings that surround it today were brought about by this highly successful fund-raising campaign.

THE MILLION DOLLAR CAMPAIGN

The plan for Denny's Million Dollar campus was produced in 1925 by Kessler and Schillinger, Birmingham landscape architects. In many respects similar to the earlier Greater University Plan, it consisted of major classroom buildings along the sides of the Quadrangle, the south edge of which was formed by University Boulevard, the east by Sixth Avenue, the west by Ninth Avenue (now Colonial Drive), and the north by Capstone Drive. Traffic circles were to define the intersections of these roads. But since University Boulevard was both a federal highway and a major thoroughfare through Tuscaloosa, traffic could not be obstructed on it, and the idea of traffic circles at the southern entrance of the campus had to be abandoned. However, in the following years architects built three of the four proposed buildings with ceremonial corner entrances. Such devices were favorite Beaux-Arts methods for emphasizing important intersections of major axes in a formal plan.

In the 1925 plan the proposed location of a new library, a top priority in the earlier scheme and this one, was moved northward from the ruins of the Rotunda to the center of the Old Quadrangle. The Victorian buildings, almost universally reviled in the 1920s, were to be demolished. The original 1831 road bisecting the Quadrangle and defining the major north-south axis of the campus was to be the approach to the proposed new library. Its north facade would form the southern edge of a smaller quadrangle bounded by Comer Hall [18] and a new building on the west and two new buildings on the east. The Louisville & Nashville railroad with a university station formed the northern edge. The station had long been demolished when the tracks were finally removed in the 1970s.

The development of the women's campus located south of University Boulevard and west of the President's Mansion [4] marked another change from the earlier plan. Segregation of the sexes (on separate campuses in many instances) was common practice in American colleges and universities until the second half of the twentieth century. In the Million Dollar Plan, clusters of sorority houses, small

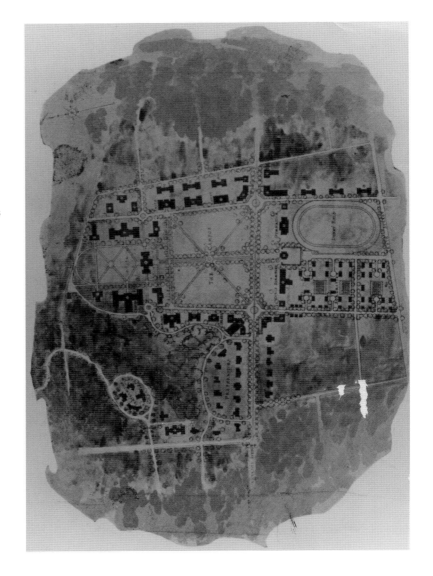

dormitories, and faculty houses were envisioned in the area immediately south of Tutwiler Hall [22] (now the site of Rose Administration Building [35]) and on either side of Colonial Drive.

When Denny became president in 1912, he urged the board of trustees to allow fraternities to build chapter houses on campus. Until then, these organizations had rented houses in town or in neighborhoods near the university. Both the 1906 Greater University Plan and the Million Dollar Plan made provisions for an isolated circle of chapter houses on the western edge of campus, but this site was later used for the construction of faculty houses. The first on-campus fraternity house was built in 1914 on University Boulevard, which became the preferred location for chapter houses for many decades. The construction of the gymnasium, Little Hall [23a], next to the President's Mansion [4], opened the area behind for sports activities. Named Denny Field, it was used for football games until the construction of Denny Stadium [103] in 1929. It continued to be used as a sports field until women's dormitories were built on the site during the late 1950s and early 1960s.

Public Works Administration Funds

The Great Depression of the 1930s slowed the construction of many of the proposed buildings in the Million Dollar Plan. However, Public Works Administration (PWA) funds became available in the late 1930s and work was resumed. By 1939 the university was in the process of spending in excess of $2 million on the construction of fourteen new structures. These included Foster Auditorium [32], the Amelia Gayle Gorgas Library [24], six men's dormitories (Presidential Dormitories [48], demolished in 2010), New Hall (a women's dormitory), a new engineering laboratory building, additions to Bidgood [44] and Bibb Graves [41] halls, an addition to the Women's Dining Hall, and a new Bath House at the swimming pool located next to Marr's Spring [7]. PWA funds were responsible for 45 percent of the money while the university supplied the remaining 55 percent.

The portion of campus north of the Louisville & Nashville railroad that once ran on an east–west axis through campus had been used for farming by the nineteenth-century university community. In 1939 it was developed into twenty one-story houses for male students and officially named Ridgecrest. When substantial new brick dormitories (now demolished) were built in this area in the late 1940s and early 1950s, many of these old PWA buildings were removed, although several of them survived as storehouses until the 1970s. The topography of this part of campus was completely transformed in the first decade of the twenty-first century with the construction of a series of large student residential communities [70].

Meantime, in the 1950s, new fraternity houses were constructed on University Boulevard east of the Quadrangle. And in the 1960s, additional chapter houses were added nearby along a new road, Jefferson Avenue, then called "New Fraternity Row."

Postwar Construction

The Second World War stopped building on the university campus, but the decade after the conflict was a time of expansion because new buildings were needed to accommodate the hordes of veterans who returned to school on the GI Bill.

The "Veterans Emergency Housing Program" carried out on campus from 1945 to 1948 involved the installation of war surplus and army establishment buildings secured from various government agencies. By 1949 scores of prefabricated structures dismantled from military bases were erected in residential areas of campus.

Three permanent academic buildings were also erected during this era. Gallalee [28] and Houser [52] halls filled in the two remaining sites of the 1925 plan. The Music and Speech Building (now Rowand-Johnson Hall) [50] was the last major building to be constructed before the school's 125th anniversary and the first structure to deviate in its placement from the Million Dollar Plan.

Architects

A number of architects built structures on the university campus between 1914 and 1956. Among them was Tuscaloosa architect E. J. Ostling, who in 1914 built a now-demolished chapter house for Phi Gamma Delta, the first fraternity to erect a house on campus.

Birmingham architect D. O. Whilldin designed five fraternity houses and one sorority house between 1916 and 1925. All have been razed. His imposing Delta Kappa Epsilon house (1916), long a campus landmark on University Boulevard, survived until 2006, when it was demolished to provide space for the expansion of the north entrance to Bryant-Denny Stadium [103]. Whilldin's Druid City Hospital (later used as the university infirmary) has also been razed, but his adjacent Nurses' Home [30] still survives.

In 1917 Birmingham architects William T. Warren and Eugene H. Knight designed a now-demolished house for the Kappa Alpha fraternity—their first commission at the Capstone. Later, as Warren, Knight, and Davis, they built three large campus structures: Lloyd Hall [26] (1927), Bibb Graves Hall [41] (1929), and Barnwell Hall

[38] (1931). The firm also designed several buildings at Bryce Hospital, including the Women's Reception Building [77] (1939).

The vast majority of the buildings erected on the University of Alabama campus in the first half of the twentieth century were built by the Birmingham firm Miller, Martin, and Lewis. By 1952 when Hugh Martin retired from active practice, his firm had built on the Alabama campus thirty-nine academic buildings and sports facilities, eighteen chapter houses for fraternities and sororities, and ten faculty houses. It had also remodeled the Victorian buildings on the Old Quad. During this period Warren, Knight, and Davis exercised a similar monopoly over campus construction at the Alabama Polytechnic Institute (now Auburn University).

John Alexander Miller, the oldest member of the Miller, Martin, and Lewis firm, was born in Glasgow, Scotland, in 1862. He studied at the University of London and spent several years designing government buildings in South Africa before coming to the United States, where he worked in architectural offices in Philadelphia and New York. At the turn of the century Miller moved to Birmingham, Alabama, forming a partnership with Hugh Martin with whom he had worked in the New York office of R. H. Robertson.

Hugh Martin, born in Paducah, Kentucky, in 1874, graduated in architecture at Cornell in 1894, where he was a member of Alpha Tau Omega. His affiliation with that society probably initiated his firm's first contract at the university in 1917 when the Alabama chapter of the fraternity selected "Brother Martin" from Birmingham to build their chapter house. In later life Martin was particularly proud of his work at the university and considered the Student Union (now Reese Phifer Hall [40]) and the Amelia Gayle Gorgas Library [24] to be among the best works of his career. Martin retired from the firm in 1952 and died in 1959.

James Artemis Lewis, born in 1890 in Columbus, Georgia, attended school in Atlanta. He became a partner with Miller and Martin in 1914 and remained with the firm until his death in 1958. Although Miller retired from the firm in 1930, Martin and Lewis retained his name because they felt "that the real foundations of the firm's practice were his responsibility, and should be his credit."

In 1940 Edwin T. McCowan joined the firm, which was eventually renamed McCowan and Knight. During the first half of the twentieth century, Miller, Martin, and Lewis designed over four thousand structures, among which were many buildings at the University of Alabama and in the Tuscaloosa community.

The University of Alabama's growth during the last half of the twentieth and first decade of the twenty-first century has been keyed to milestones in its history coupled with highly successful capital campaigns that enabled the institution to erect costly new buildings on campus.

125th Anniversary

In 1956, as the university community prepared to celebrate its 125th anniversary, planners were busy projecting its future needs. At the time the campus provided adequate classroom facilities for almost all of the schools and colleges around the main and old quadrangles. Yet it was clear that new buildings would have to be provided in the future for the growth of existing programs and any additions to them. The Music and Speech Building (now Rowand-Johnson Hall [50]), had opened only the year before, the first major academic building constructed since the completion of the 1925 master plan. The problems of building it in such a challenging location exemplified the difficulties the university faced before the Urban Redevelopment Program, the Bryce Hospital land swap, and the later purchase of the hospital itself, greatly enlarged the size of the campus.

The most important building needs in 1956 were additional student housing and a new athletic field house. The construction of these buildings hinged on the athletic facility to be built on Thomas Field, for with the removal of athletic offices from Moore Hall [23b], it would then be possible to renovate that building and Little Hall [23a] for academic purposes. Denny Field, directly behind them, and the area south of Foster Auditorium [32], then being used by the Athletic Department, were slated to be part of the expanded women's campus. Some progress was made in implementing the plans during the next several years, but it was not until the early 1960s that the largest of the women's dormitory complexes, Mary Burke and Martha Parham halls [33], were constructed in these areas.

The 1956 plan also called for further development of Ridgecrest near the Black Warrior River. Several men's dormitories (now demolished) replaced some of the PWA and postwar wooden structures in that area.

The Greater University Development Campaign

In 1959 President Frank A. Rose launched the "Greater University Development Campaign." Its initial goal was to raise at least $5 million to fund such "bed-rock essentials as new faculty, new equipment, and an engineering building program (needed to satisfy accreditation requirements)." A new wing for Lloyd Hall [26] was also a top priority. This capital campaign became the first phase of a highly successful decade-long fund drive. Funds from it, added to the university's share of a state bond issue of $100 million for capital outlay, plus loans from the College Housing Loan Program, made possible much of the new construction on campus.

The General Development Plan

In the meantime it became apparent that a new master plan was needed to direct and control the growth and expansion of the campus. In 1961 Olmstead Associates, landscape architects from Brookline, Massachusetts, completed the "General Development Plan," which called for clusters of buildings associated with related disciplines.

The liberal arts group was to include the buildings of the Old Quadrangle, the Music and Speech Building (now Rowand-Johnson Hall [50]), Comer Hall [18] (to be renovated for use by the College of Arts and Sciences), and two new buildings, ten Hoor Hall [49] and a structure north of Comer Hall.

Hardaway Hall [51], Houser Hall [52], and four new buildings were to serve engineering. One of these, the Mineral Industries Building [53], also known as the Hugh Moss Comer Hall, was the first structure of the new plan to be built.

The proposed science complex included several new buildings directly behind the eastern edge of the Quadrangle. The Biology Building [60] and the mathematics-psychology building, Gordon Palmer Hall [63], were planned as part of this group.

Urban Redevelopment Project

In 1959 the university also entered into negotiations with the city of Tuscaloosa and the federal government to redevelop a run-down residential neighborhood on the southeastern edge of campus between Hackberry Lane, University Boulevard, and 10th Street (now Bryant Drive). Residents of this area were relocated, some being given the option of moving into a nearby housing project (now the site of the university Police Department [90]). This redevelopment was a gradual process, and the land did not become available to the university until several years later. Nevertheless, it eventually had a significant impact on the development of the campus in the 1980s.

The Bryce Hospital Land Swap

Throughout the 1960s the development of the university campus was hampered by lack of available space for new construction. In the latter part of the decade, however, negotiations were begun with Bryce Hospital to acquire a portion of that historic institution's extensive land holdings. The hospital, created by an act of the legislature in 1852, was located on land adjacent to the University of Alabama. For more than a century Bryce patients had farmed it as part of their treatment. But new labor acts prohibited such therapy and Bryce no longer needed the land. By the 1960s the hospital was severely overcrowded and in financial difficulties. The university did not have the money to buy the Bryce property, but it was able to negotiate an exchange of the Northington Campus, a World War II army hospital complex granted to the university by the federal government, together with a tract of land near Birmingham, for portions of the Bryce property adjoining the university campus. This exchange would allow the hospital to lease or sell the swapped land and thus ease its financial situation, while the university would expand its campus by more than 50 percent.

Plans for using the land gained by the Urban Redevelopment Program and the land swap began immediately. The area the university acquired was divided into three segments, or campuses. The original campus was designated "No. 1" and remained the traditional residential core of the institution. "Campus No. 2," located closest to the original campus, was to be developed with the proposed Law Center [92] and a complex later named the Paul W. Bryant Conference Center [93]. Over the following decade this "campus" was expanded to include the Frank M. Moody Music Building [91]. "Campus No. 3," nearest DCH Regional Medical Center [85], was developed for health-related fields. A portion of this campus addition

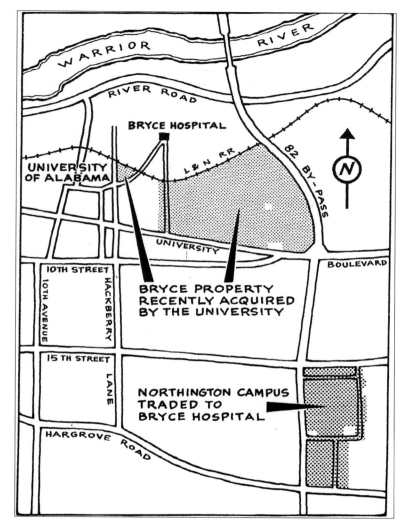

WARRIOR RIVER

RIVER ROAD

BRYCE HOSPITAL

UNIVERSITY OF ALABAMA

L & N RR

82 BY-PASS

N

UNIVERSITY

10TH STREET

10TH AVENUE

HACKBERRY

BOULEVARD

BRYCE PROPERTY RECENTLY ACQUIRED BY THE UNIVERSITY

15 TH STREET

LANE

NORTHINGTON CAMPUS TRADED TO BRYCE HOSPITAL

HARGROVE ROAD

FIGURE 16 University of Alabama–Bryce Hospital Land Swap, 1971. Acquisition of adjacent hospital property allowed for campus expansion in the last quarter of the twentieth century.

University of Alabama Alumni Bulletin (Winter 1971): 24, 1.

was later utilized for the University of Alabama System Office [89] and various sports, including soccer, tennis, softball, and the Student Recreation Center [102].

Sesquicentennial Capital Campaign

The university reached its 150th anniversary in 1981 during the presidency of Dr. Joab L. Thomas. As part of the celebration of this milestone, the institution undertook a three-year "Sesquicentennial Capital Campaign," which raised $62 million and resulted in the eventual construction of the Paul W. Bryant Conference Center [93], the Frank M. Moody Music Building [91], and the Bevill Building [54].

1985 Campus Master Plan

In 1984, as this capital campaign was drawing to a close, the board of trustees of the University of Alabama System requested that the Tuscaloosa, Birmingham, and Huntsville campuses formulate and adopt master plans for improvement and future development. In Tuscaloosa a committee began work with Woolpert Consultants of Dayton, Ohio, and Mobile, and Almon Associates Inc. of Tuscaloosa to develop a plan. Planners pointed out the serious impact the automobile-oriented culture of the 1960s and 1970s had had upon the beauty and character of the original urban and pedestrian-oriented campus. Tentative corrective measures included reducing the number of cars allowed to park in central campus by banning parking entirely on University Boulevard and by removing some parking from the sides of the Quadrangle. The most dramatic suggestion (that took fifteen years to accomplish) was to close McCorvey Drive at the Ferguson Center [64] and create a pedestrian walkway and plaza. Other suggestions in this plan that were eventually carried out were the removal of the physical plant from the Ridgecrest area and the construction of student residential communities on this site.

University Neighborhood Plan

In addition to developing a campus master plan, the university, in partnership with the city of Tuscaloosa, hired Woolpert Consultants in 1990 to address the long-standing problems faced by neighborhoods adjacent to the campus. Unfortunately, developers were opposed to any attempt to regulate the construction of multiunit apartments and condominiums in what had once been single-family neighborhoods, and the proposed University Neighborhood Plan known as the "Buffer Zone Plan" never became a reality. It took another decade and further deterioration of these neighborhoods before compromises with developers brought some order and stability to these areas adjacent to campus.

Campaign for Alabama

The 1985 Campus Master Plan was updated at the beginning of the "Campaign for Alabama," a capital campaign initiated during the presidency of Dr. Andrew A. Sorensen. Six years later in 1999, a year after the completion of this campaign that had raised $224 million, it

was again updated and expanded to address the changing needs of the university. Among the new buildings that eventually resulted from this capital campaign were the Bruno Library and Bashinsky Computer Center [46], Alston Hall [45], the AIME Building [55], and Shelby Hall [56].

Our Students, Our Future

Under the leadership of Dr. Robert E. Witt, who became the university's president in 2003, the institution underwent dramatic changes, the likes of which had not been seen since the Denny years over eighty years earlier. In his speech to the faculty and staff that fall, Dr. Witt laid out his "Vision for the University," which he declared could be used as a "roadmap for progress" in the twenty-first century. Among the goals President Witt set forth were increasing enrollment with high quality students and strengthening the academic and research reputation of the institution. To fund these he initiated a new capital campaign, "Our Students, Our Future." At its conclusion in 2009, it had brought in a record-breaking $612 million.

The Witt plan called for the enrollment of 28,000 students by

FIGURE 17 Campus Master Plan, 1985. The University of Alabama System board of trustees mandated that all three campuses adopt master plans for improvement and expansion. At Tuscaloosa planners studied the impact of the 1960s and 1970s automobile culture on campus and initiated plans to return it to a more urban and pedestrian-oriented environment.

Courtesy of the W. S. Hoole Special Collections Library, the University of Alabama.

2013. This goal was reached years earlier than expected in September 2009, when the university enrolled 28,807 students. By the fall of 2012 a record-breaking 33,602 students signed up for classes. Just as in the Denny years during the last century, increased enrollment necessitated the construction of new residence halls and dining facilities, the renovation of older ones, and permitting fraternities and sororities to expand or to build new and larger chapter houses on campus.

2007 Campus Master Plan

With so many changes taking place, it became evident that a new master plan, reflecting the present and future needs of a vastly larger institution, was needed. In 2005 KPS Group, Inc., of Birmingham headed the planning effort in conjunction with the university's Planning Department and created not just another master plan but also a much-needed Design Guide that set standards and made suggestions for architects and contractors building structures on campus. One dilemma the planners faced was determining how to retain the intimacy and coherence of the central campus in a vastly larger complex. They attempted to accomplish this by employing New Urbanist ideas such as creating clusters of neighborhoods, each possessing a diversity of residential, academic, and public amenities. A key factor in making this concept work was the introduction of the Crimson Ride bus system in 2007, which connects all parts of campus. A tram system had been initiated in January 1978, but the open-sided cars proved unpopular, especially in inclement weather, and this novel transportation experiment lasted for only about one year.

2010 Bryce Hospital Purchase

The State of Alabama Department of Mental Health sold the remaining portions of the Bryce Hospital campus to the University of Alabama in May 2010. The consequences of this sale on the future development of the school are enormous. Utilization of the land and of the historic hospital buildings offers both a challenge and an exciting opportunity.

Looking Forward

In the first decade of the twenty-first century, despite a major recession, the University of Alabama grew at a phenomenal pace. As

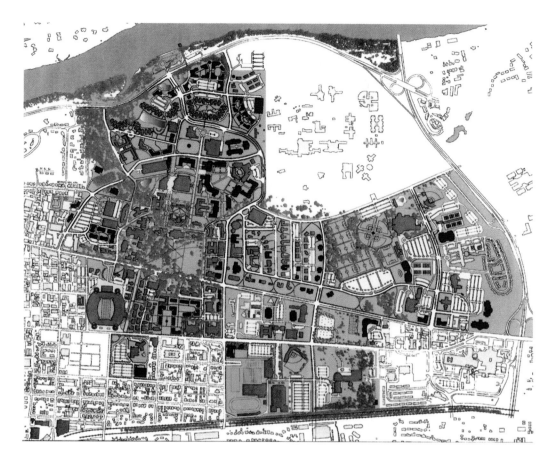

this guide goes to press plans are being made for the future use of the former Bryce campus and its buildings, new structures are currently being built, and others are in the planning stages. An administrator recently observed that for the past five years the university began construction of a new building every three months! As a result, alumni returning to their alma mater will discover that the campus of their school days has been transformed dramatically. Its sheer size may at first appear daunting, but most visitors will agree that the campus has never appeared more beautiful. The university's 182-year track record of methodical (if not always effective) planning has paid off. It is encouraging to note that current planners and designers have paid careful attention to earlier campus plans, learned from their mistakes, and have adopted design standards, policies, and procedures that should, if followed, provide a sturdy framework for twenty-first-century campus growth. The updated master plan calls for the con-

FIGURE 18 Campus Master Plan, 2007. Tremendous growth in the first years of the twenty-first century required yet another master plan to address a wide variety of complex and challenging issues. Purchase of the remaining portions of the Bryce Hospital campus in 2010 required an update to the plan in 2012.

struction of new state-of-the-art buildings as needed, but it also gives emphasis to the need to respect and preserve the historic architecture and traditions of the familiar older areas of campus that give the university its unique character and sense of place.

ARCHITECTURAL STYLES

Like many other builders of the 1960s and early 1970s, architects of new campus structures in those years ignored the Classical Revival buildings from the first half of the twentieth century and created modern structures that made no reference to traditional architecture. However, vocal opposition from alumni and the general public caused the board of trustees to reconsider the design of some of the projected central campus buildings, with the result that the proposed facade of the Rose Administration Building [35] was considerably altered to make it "fit in," and columns were added to the design of the Biology Building [60]. The Modernist design of Ferguson Center [64] was not altered, but due to protests, its original location was changed to spare historic Woods Hall [11]. Buildings in Modern styles were built on the periphery of campus, including the now-demolished Rose Towers [68], Tutwiler Hall [72], the Family Practice Clinic of the College of Health Sciences (now the Speech and Hearing Center) [81], and the Law Center [92].

Fraternities and sororities, for the most part, as might be expected, continued to erect new houses designed in conservative and traditional styles. The most unusual chapter house of that era was designed in 1964 by Birmingham architect Lawrence Whitten for the Sigma Nu Fraternity—a recreation of the Governor's Palace in Williamsburg. By the end of the twentieth century Modernism had been on the decline for over two decades on the national level, yet Modern style structures like the Bevill Building [54] continued to be built on the Alabama campus into the early 1980s. The favored style of that decade was Postmodernism, a movement that reflected the growing pluralism in architecture and was actually not one style but many, some of which revealed a renewed interest in classicism. One such variant style, termed "Ironic Classicism" by the architect and critic Robert A. M. Stern, in his 1988 *Modern Classicism,* first appeared on campus in the Frank M. Moody Music Building [91]. In this style historically based elements could be included once again in architecture, but always with irony, or, as it were, "in quotation marks." Unfortunately, as Stern pointed out, "in the hands of many ironists, architecture becomes a matter of built jokes, and nothing goes flat faster than a joke." One wonders, in fact, how many visitors to the university who view such Ironic Classical structures as the Frank M. Moody Music Building [91] and the Rodgers Library [59] understand the irony or "get the jokes."

Stern identified another Postmodernist classical variation as "Modern Traditionalism." Such buildings combine modern design and construction with classical elements that are used freely, but neither jokingly nor literally. This stylistic designation appears appropriate for many of the campus buildings erected since the late 1980s.

A third variation of Classical Postmodernism mentioned by Stern, "Canonic or Archaeological Classicism," also referred to as "Neo-Traditionalism," is best represented in Tuscaloosa by the new Federal Building and Courthouse (completed 2011) on University Boulevard and designed by Chicago-based HBRA Architects. Architects working in this style attempt to continue the classical tradition following the paradigms of Palladio, Vignola, Robert Adam, and others, with as little deviation as possible. On the University of Alabama campus the Bruno Library and Bashinsky Computer Center [46], Shelby Hall [56], buildings in the Science and Engineering Research Complex [57], and the Capstone College of Nursing [84] exhibit rather tentative interpretations of this "Neo-Traditional" style. In some respects the architects of these buildings also come closest to resurrecting the aesthetic of the early twentieth-century architects working on campus. This is particularly notable in the Capstone College of Nursing with its dramatic location and corner entrance that evokes (minus the dome and much of the subtlety) Miller, Martin, and Lewis's 1930 Union Building (now Reese Phifer Hall) [40].

TOUR 1   ANTEBELLUM CAMPUS TOUR

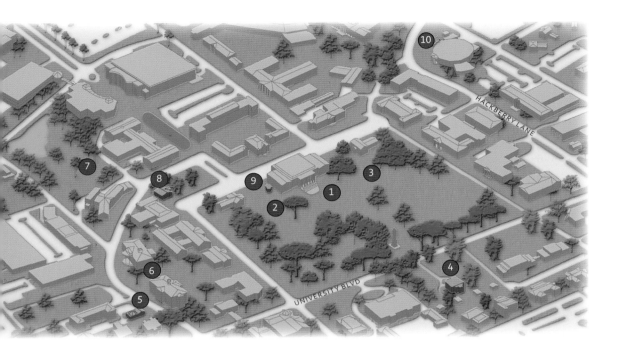

1   ROTUNDA

2   MOUND

3   FOUNDATIONS

4   PRESIDENT'S MANSION

5   MAXWELL HALL (OBSERVATORY)

6   STUDENT FORTIFICATIONS (DESTROYED)

7   MARR'S SPRING

8   GORGAS HOUSE

9   GUARD HOUSE

10   CEMETERY

36

1 ROTUNDA

The semicircular plaza in front of the Gorgas Library [24] marks the location of the southern half of the antebellum university's library, the Rotunda, designed by architect William Nichols. Flagstones embedded in the aggregate indicate the perimeter and internal features of the building as revealed in a 1984 archaeological excavation of the site. The bronze plaque at the foot of the steps bears a representation of the original University of Alabama seal. Buried below it is a time capsule scheduled to be opened in 2031, the university's bicentennial. The foundations of the northern half of this circular structure are obscured by the massive stone steps of the 1939 library, symbolically positioned so that they would rest exactly upon the foundations of the main walls of the Rotunda.

The building was still incomplete on April 18, 1831, when the University of Alabama officially opened. (For additional information on this era, see "The Antebellum Campus, 1828–65," p. 1.) Like Thomas Jefferson's rotunda at the University of Virginia, the design of the Alabama Rotunda reflects the ancient Roman Pantheon. Jefferson and Nichols, each inspired by Andrea Palladio's detailed engravings of this Roman building, transformed the circular Pantheon—a temple dedicated to all the gods—into a temple of learning, that is, a library. Each architect made his library the nucleus of an ideal scholarly community.

Today we can visualize the proportions of Nichol's library by observing the flagstones imbedded in the plaza and by examining a conjectural cross section of the building. Above ground the Rotunda was constructed of brick, stone, and wood. Its most prominent features were the large classical dome covered with wooden shingles and rising 72 feet above the campus (Nichols's building, like Jefferson's, was designed to be one-half the scale of the Pantheon), and its exterior colonnade of twenty-four paired Ionic columns. Nichols's choice of the Ionic order for both the Rotunda and the nearby Lyceum is interesting. Like many architects, Nichols, a Mason, would have been familiar with that society's beliefs about the distinctive virtues expressed by the classical orders: Doric proclaims strength, Corinthian expresses beauty, and Ionic symbolizes wisdom. The bases and capitals of the Rotunda columns were carved of local sandstone, while their shafts were made of special wedge-shaped bricks stuccoed to imitate cut stone. The location of these paired columns can be seen in the additional rectangular reinforcements on the inside of the exterior ring of the foundations. Several of

Above: Archaeological excavation of the Rotunda, 1984

Rght: Conjectural cross-section of the Rotunda

the Ionic capitals and a few of the special column bricks from the building have been preserved and are now housed in the W. S. Hoole Special Collections Library.

Conjectural rendering of the Rotunda's south façade

The main entrance to the Rotunda [1] faced south toward the Huntsville Road (University Boulevard), and the avenue leading to it was lined with cedar trees. One entered the structure through a shallow porch into a foyer containing a staircase to the upper floor under the dome. The ground floor held a large circular two-story commencement hall and chapel surrounded by an interior colonnade of twelve Corinthian columns. Rectangular flagstone footings of six of these columns may be seen in the plaza. A speaker's stand was placed on a low stage between two of the columns, a stage that also contained a wooden bench for members of the faculty. Students sat on benches according to class rank. Visitors were also seated on the remaining benches and in Windsor chairs in the balcony encircling the hall. Two flagstone rectangles between the foundations for the inner colonnade and the outer wall probably were the footings for curving stairs that led to the balcony.

The dome room, containing the university's library and natural history collection, was apparently accessible only from the staircase in the foyer.

Doors at the top of the stairs could be locked to secure the valuable collections. Specially designed bookshelves with lower cabinets for natural history specimens lined the walls. The enormous room was heated—albeit inadequately—by at least two fireplaces embedded in the massive brick walls.

The dome room was probably one of the most beautiful architectural spaces in the South, but it was far from practical as a library. Students soon discovered the fascinating properties of domed interiors: words spoken in an ordinary tone of voice seemed to break into fragments, but whispers could be clearly heard from one end of the room to the other. Books "accidentally" dropped at strategic locations could produce heart-stopping bangs followed by shattering reverberations. Pranks and vandalism were commonplace in the antebellum period. Many of them were focused on the Rotunda, where daily attendance at chapel was strictly enforced. In 1848 all the doorknobs were broken off. In other incidents that year whiskey bottles and playing cards were placed on the rostrum and oil was poured on the faculty bench. The library was also mistreated. To gain access to it, students climbed out of the windows in the stairwell onto the roof of the colonnade and then into windows of the dome room. Books were disarranged and stuffed birds and mammals were removed from their cases and comically arranged around the roof of the structure. Students also managed to hoist a two-year-old calf up to the roof and tether it to a lightning rod attached to the apex of the dome. The harassed faculty had had enough. Iron bars were placed over the stair hall windows and for good measure the windows were nailed shut. Natural history specimens were to be kept under lock and key, and a special wire mesh was ordered in 1852 from New York to cover the bookcases. ("Spit boxes," i.e., spittoons, were also ordered to protect the library floors from defilement.) Access to books was permitted only at certain hours and under the careful supervision of the librarian in charge. The lower floor of the Rotunda was also refurbished in the early 1850s and its use restricted. President Basil Manly determined to hold daily chapel services in the nearby Lyceum and to reserve the Rotunda auditorium for commencement services only.

The actual number of books housed in the library is not known. Accounts vary considerably, but at the time of its destruction by fire on April 4, 1865, the library may have contained as many as 7,000 volumes. According to tradition, only one book, an 1853 English translation of the *Koran,* escaped the flames. In actual fact, at least 1,200 books were saved. Some of these volumes now preserved in the W. S. Hoole Special Collections Library are charred around the edges and still smell of smoke. Others were undoubtedly in nearby faculty houses that were spared destruction. Almost all of the natural history collections were destroyed, although some specimens were salvaged from the ruins after the fire.

The Boulder

The United Daughters of the Confederacy (UDC) dedicated the large stone marker south of the Rotunda Plaza in 1914 to the memory of all University of Alabama students who served in the Civil War. The marker originally stood in the center of the site of the Rotunda, but with the construction of the Gorgas Library in 1939 it was moved to the south. The university gave the Confederacy 7 generals, 25 colonels, 14 lieutenant colonels, 21 majors, 125 captains, 273 staff and other commissioned officers, 66 noncommissioned officers, and 294 privates.

Memorial Plaques

Two other memorials dedicated to university cadets who served in this war may be viewed at the top of the Gorgas Library steps under the portico. As James B. Sellers pointed out in his 1953 *History of the University of Alabama,* both markers are dedicated to "deserters," that is, cadets whose "impatient patriotism" caused them to leave the university before graduating. One bronze plaque commemorates Captain Charles P. Storrs's cadet troop made up of university students and young men from Montgomery. The other memorial commemorates the nineteen university cadets in Captain Bascom T. Shockly's escort company of cavalry.

Memorial Window

The most imposing and beautiful memorial to the university's participation in this tragic conflict is a stained glass window designed by Tiffany Studios of New York that was once located in the Gorgas Library but is now on display in the W. S. Hoole Special Collections Library in Mary Harmon Bryant Hall [62]. The United Daughters of the Confederacy originally placed it in the first Amelia Gayle Gorgas Library (now Carmichael Hall [43]) in 1925.

The side panels of this tripartite window are geometrical in design and each contains two symbolic medallions. The upper left portrays the battle flag of the Confederacy crossed with the Alabama state flag. The lower left illustrates a cotton boll, in the points of which appear the words "dare," "love,"

Tiffany memorial
window

"pray," and "think." The upper right medallion contains the Confederate flag crossed with the Alabama state flag, while in the lower right is the badge of the UDC. At the bottom of the left panel is inscribed the dictum: *Suaviter in modo fortiter in re* (Gently in manner, strongly in deed). The lower right panel contains the inscription *Dulce et decorum est pro patria mori* (It is sweet and seemly to die for one's country).

In the central panel is a representation of "the Christian Soldier," standing erect, clad in armor of gold, his head held high. Across his shoulders is flung a crimson-lined cloak, and upon his head there rests a crown of laurel, replacing the golden helmet that he bears in one hand with his sword. His other hand rests upon his broad shield of burnished gold in which the cross is embossed. The inscription below this figure reads:

> As crusaders of old they fought their heritage to save. To the Cadets of April 3, 1865 and to Confederate soldier-students of the University 1860–65. Placed by the Alabama Division United Daughters of the Confederacy, A.D. 1925. Con Amore.

2 MOUND

The "mound," actually a pile of rubble from Franklin Hall, one of the original dormitories, is associated with the traditional tapping ceremonies of the Jasons and Mortar Board honor societies. It has also served as the stage for countless group photographs of various campus organizations for well over a century. Franklin Hall was the third dormitory to be constructed. Washington and Jefferson halls had been completed in time for the official opening of the university in April 1831. The foundations of Washington Hall (just north of Oliver-Barnard Hall [16]) and Jefferson Hall (just north of Tuomey Hall [15]) are buried below the pavement of Capstone Drive. These two dorms were designed to house ninety-six students. According to a contemporary description, each building was constructed in a "plain, but durable style of architecture" and was "divided into 12 compartments of three rooms each, being one sitting room in front, with a fire place, and two bedrooms behind. Each of the compartments [could] accommodate 4 students." Portions of both dormitories were excavated in archaeological digs during the summer of 2007. Objects recovered include charred furniture and belongings of the last students to inhabit these dormitories before Union forces torched them.

Anticipating an increase in enrollment, the board of trustees in 1832 authorized the architect, William Nichols, to provide a set of plans for a third, and larger, dormitory to be built to the south of Washington Hall. Franklin Hall was completed the following year. But since the projected increases in enrollment did not occur, these additional rooms made it possible for two, rather than four, students to share a "compartment." Enrollment, in fact, remained quite low before 1860, averaging only about ninety-six students a year. Extra "compartments" were used throughout the antebellum period for various purposes including additional faculty housing. Federal troops burned Franklin Hall on April 4, 1865.

Above: Mound

Right: Drawing of the ruins of Franklin Hall by Eugene Allen Smith, 1865

3 FOUNDATIONS

Opposite the Rotunda [1] and corresponding to Franklin Hall is a brick marker indicating the location of Madison Hall, the last of the four dormitories to be constructed according to Nichols's plan. Built in 1859, Madison Hall was designed by a faculty committee to conform in its external appearance to Franklin Hall toward which it faced. The interior contained meeting halls for the Erosophic and Philomathic literary societies and rooms for their extensive libraries as well as dormitory rooms for students. In the 1860s the building was enlarged with the addition of a mess hall for cadets.

The four dormitories sufficed to meet the needs of the school until 1863 when the university, for the first time in its history, experienced a tremendous increase in enrollment. To meet the demand, President Garland ordered two very crude barracks to be constructed between the dormitories on the present sites of Tuomey [15] and Oliver-Barnard [16] halls. Although cadets later dignified these structures with the titles of Johnson and Lee barracks, President Garland in his letter book referred to them as temporary "shanties" built "in the cheapest manner possible & out of lumber sawed for fencing, of such lengths as to be useful hereafter for fencing which the Unty grounds are always in need of."

The dormitories and barracks were destroyed with almost all other structures on the campus during the April 4, 1865, Federal raid. Usable material from the ruined buildings was salvaged soon after the war, but much of the debris was left on the site. For many years the center of the campus was a litter-strewn field overgrown with weeds. Despite its shabby appearance, the site was the object of strong feelings. A decade after the burning of the campus, a writer for the April 29, 1875, *Tuscaloosa Blade* suggested that the ruins be left as a reminder for future generations of the senseless destruction of war and the "nation's folly" for resorting to it as a means to solve its internal disputes. After yet another decade, during a campus beautification project, the ruins of the old buildings were collected into neat rectangular piles and developed as "mounds of beauty" covered with "the choicest flowers." In florid prose a student writer for the December 14, 1886, *Alabama University Monthly* expressed current sentiment: "The cry of 'vandalism' should be hushed, the traces of the ravages wrought by the rude, red hand of war should be removed, and the lips of flowers may well be made to tell the more eloquent tale of the new era of peace and prosperity."

These grassy mounds with their historic ties to the early university continued to be treasured by later generations of students. It was only after considerable protest that in 1910 all of the mounds except one were removed during the expansion of the campus. According to the May 31, 1910, *Crimson-White* this mound was saved by the actions of the law students: "The law department, whose members are more given to words than [are] other students, held a session on the mound near their building [Oliver-Barnard Hall (16)] and an all-day speaking, they say, succeeded [in preserving] that heap to posterity." Debris from the demolished mounds was used as fill behind Smith [20], Comer [18], and Morgan [19] halls. In 1975 the site of

Archeological excavation exposing the foundations of Madison Hall, 1975

Drawing of the ruins of Jefferson Hall by Eugene Allen Smith, 1865

Madison Hall was partially revealed during an archaeological excavation. Items recovered are now preserved in the W. S. Hoole Special Collections Library. Among them were a charred copy of Shakespeare's *Much Ado About Nothing,* a book on plane geometry, and a geography of Africa.

Throughout the twentieth century the open area on the eastern side of the main quadrangle was used as a drill field for ROTC units and for the site of enormous homecoming bonfires.

4 PRESIDENT'S MANSION

The President's Mansion, constructed between 1839 and 1841, was not a part of the original 1828 campus plan. Until 1841 the president and his family lived in one of the faculty houses William Nichols designed. To provide a more suitable residence for its dynamic new president, the Reverend Basil Manly, the board of trustees passed a resolution in December 1838 appropriating funds. A committee was formed and charged with the responsibility of selecting a site on campus and a suitable design for the new building. It did not have access to Nichols's plans and drawings of the campus, for he had apparently taken them with him when he left the state in 1833. As a consequence, members of the committee recorded that since they had "no plan of the original design by which they could be governed . . . it became necessary therefore to take the buildings as they stood and form such a design from them as appeared most likely to answer the great object in view."

The mansion was constructed following the plans provided by Michael Barry, a carpenter-builder who served as both architect and building superintendent. Designed on a monumental scale, it cost far more that the board of trustees had originally intended to spend. Several state legislators condemned the trustees and accused them of having misused the educational trust fund, and of having created a "palace" for the president. It had so many rooms, they contended, that he and his family would never be able to occupy all of them. The house was expensive, and it was certainly large and difficult to furnish, as Manly discovered to his regret. Before moving in he made a special trip downriver to Mobile and New Orleans to buy additional household items. On the return trip the steamer *Hercules* sank with all his new furniture on board.

In 1851 Manly had one of the large front rooms on the second floor fitted up as a session room for the board of trustees. The university had been deeded the capitol and its contents when the seat of government was moved to Montgomery, so Manly used several of the legislators' desks, tables, and chairs for furnishing this room. A number of the pieces from the capitol, custom designed by the architect to fit that building, still survive. Several are on permanent display in the W. S. Hoole Special Collections Library.

The present appearance of the President's Mansion with its snow-white columns and walls dates only from 1908 and bears little resemblance to its once-colorful nineteenth-century appearance. Paint specifications and a contemporary watercolor of the building reveal that only its facade was

The President's Mansion was painted white in 1908.

stuccoed and painted to imitate cut stone. The doors and window casings were also painted a "stone color." The doors and window frames, however, were painted white and the blinds painted green. The column shafts appear to have been buff colored, and the bases and Ionic capitals were white. The brick walls, left exposed at the sides and rear of the structure, added even more texture and color to the building. The only original ironwork, the handsome third-story wrought- and cast-iron balcony, was undoubtedly shipped upriver from Mobile or New Orleans. The cast-iron railings on the second-story porch were ordered from the Cornell Company Ironworks in New York in 1853. Matching railings for the curving stairs were also ordered, but they had to be returned because of errors in measurement. It was not until 1887 that a permanent iron railing matching that on the porches of Manly [13] and Garland [14] halls was finally put in place on the staircases.

A wooden balustrade painted white originally crowned the roof of the portico. At some point during the 1880s this was replaced with iron roof-cresting to match the ironwork on William A. Freret's new Victorian buildings on the north side of campus. This cresting was taken down in 1908

by architect Frank Lockwood, who replaced it with a parapet, itself eventually removed in the 1920s. The present balustrade was put in place in 1997. Its design is based on careful archaeological research and replicates the lost original. Funds to recreate it were provided by Jack Warner, a local industrialist who, along with his family, has been a generous benefactor of the university for over half a century. He also donated to the mansion many period pieces of furniture and works of art including the enormous marble urn located in front of it.

The mansion retains its four original dependencies or outbuildings. The outer two of these one-story brick buildings were designed as houses for the president's personal slaves. The building on the southeast nearest the house was equipped as a kitchen but now serves as a garage. The other dependency was a well- and washhouse.

According to tradition, the mansion was spared destruction by Federal troops on April 4, 1865, because of the heroism of Mrs. Garland. When her husband and the cadets marched toward town to meet the Yankees in the early hours of that day, she and her daughters fled into the woods south of

Margaret Cammer Furman painted this watercolor of the President's Mansion, 1841. The mansion was the scene of her marriage that year to Richard Furman, a university student and friend of the Manly family.

the campus near Evergreen Cemetery. Early in the morning they walked to the Alabama Insane Hospital (Bryce) [74] and sought refuge with the Peter Bryce family. On learning of the destruction of the campus, Mrs. Garland rushed back to the President's Mansion to defend her property. Other members of the family, along with the Bryces, climbed up to the dome on the hospital and witnessed the destruction of the university from that vantage point. On entering her home Mrs. Garland discovered that soldiers were looting her belongings. One of them had set fire to a large four-poster bed (some accounts say a sofa). So commanding was her presence—years of living with rowdy schoolboys must have helped her here—that the soldiers agreed to leave the house and actually helped her put out the fire.

5 Maxwell Hall (Observatory)

Science has always been an important subject in the university's curriculum, but it is largely due to Frederick A. P. Barnard, one of its most famous antebellum professors, that the school was particularly distinguished in astronomy. The Observatory was the first building of its type to be constructed in the southeast and one of the first half-dozen observatories to be constructed in the United States. As early as 1838 Professor Barnard presented plans to the board of trustees for constructing and equipping the structure. The original portion, completed in 1844, consisted of a large central portion, capped by a revolving dome 18 feet in diameter. A transit room with a north–south slit in the roof was located on the west end and the east contained a small office with a fireplace. The classroom addition on the east was not added until 1858.

The Observatory contained the latest scientific apparatus. In 1838 Barnard had warned the trustees that this equipment was costly and not readily available and that it would probably take as long as five or six years to have the astronomical instruments custom-made in London and Paris and shipped to Tuscaloosa.

In an era before modern communications it was very difficult to arrive at "standard" time, which could vary considerably from one place to another. One important apparatus located in the Observatory was a transit circle with a four-inch objective made by Troughton and Simms of London. This instrument, housed in the western part of the building, was used in establishing the correct time. The transit circle determined the meridian-crossing times of stars with known celestial coordinates, a plan that permitted ac-

Above: The Observatory was renamed Maxwell Hall in 1986.

Left: The Observatory photographed by Eugene Allen Smith, ca. 1891.

curate setting of the Observatory's two sidereal (star) and solar clocks. The transit circle no longer exists, but the clocks and other scientific apparatus once used in the Observatory are now displayed in the Hoole Special Collections Library.

During the Civil War, observations and calculations made at the Observatory were used in compiling almanacs published by the Confederacy. The building escaped destruction during the Federal raid, but its effectiveness was severely impaired. President L. C. Garland described the results of the raid in the final entry in the Observatory's transit log: "The Observatory was forced open—all of its instruments were more or less injured, and many rendered entirely useless. One or two of the eye-pieces of the Transit were carried away, together with the collimating eye-piece. The other lenses including the object lens were saved and sent for safe keeping to the Lunatic Asylum."

According to tradition the Observatory was saved from destruction by Mrs. Reuben Chapman, who lived nearby. It is said she persuaded the Yankees that the building and its contents had not contributed "in any way to promote the spirit of rebellion among the people of the South."

Many of the damaged instruments were put back in use in later years, including the custom-designed brass equatorial telescope. In the months following the destruction of the campus, the Observatory—the only surviving public building and one of the few structures left with a good roof—was used to store the damaged collection of books, records, and equipment salvaged from the ruins. However, the devastation of the rest of the university and the extreme poverty of the state restricted the use of the scientific apparatus. Years passed before the school regained its prewar prosperity, and many decades passed before it regained its eminent position in scientific research.

In 1986 the old Observatory was named Maxwell Hall in honor of retired university consulting engineer Fred R. Maxwell Jr., who, perhaps more than any other individual, was responsible for protecting and preserving the remnants of the nineteenth-century campus. It now serves as the home of the Creative Campus Initiative.

6 STUDENT FORTIFICATIONS (DESTROYED)

The earthworks or rifle pits once located behind the Observatory [5] near the western entrance to the campus were constructed in 1863 (see fig. 13). President Garland was convinced that fortification of the campus was a matter of top priority. He knew that because the university had functioned as a military school for the Confederacy, it could expect no mercy if Federal troops ever reached Tuscaloosa. In a letter to Governor John Gill Shorter, May 7, 1863, Garland warned that "if the enemy should ever reach this place, they would not leave at this Unty one brick standing upon another." To make matters worse, he did not trust the citizens of Tuscaloosa. The majority of voters had voted against secession, and he doubted that, if pressed, they would come to the aid of the university in case of attack. Later, Garland persuaded Governor Thomas H. Watts to authorize the fortification of the campus. An agent was commissioned to impress 150 laborers, Johnson and Lee "barracks" were begun (see Foundations [3]), and thousands of wooden pickets were cut and prepared. Work was soon stopped, however, when angry Tuscaloosans sent a petition to the governor complaining that their slaves and tools, requisitioned for use by the university, were needed for work on their own crops.

The only portion of the earthworks completed before the Yankee invasion on April 4, 1865, proved to be more hazardous to students than to the Yankees. Years later, James Gillespie Cowan, in the 1901 *Alabama University Bulletin,* recalled that he and other cadets had engaged in a skirmish with the Yankees that had left several people wounded, among them Captain John Murfee, brother of Colonel James T. Murfee, commandant of cadets, who was shot in the foot. The commandant ordered Cowan and his comrades to carry the wounded man to the Owens's home on East Margin Street (now 815 17th Avenue in the Druid City Historic District). Cowan then tried to rejoin his fellow cadets. Unable to find them and thoroughly unnerved, he hurried back toward the university, moving, he recalled, "at a pace which would have rendered a professional sprinter green with envy." Unfortunately, in his haste he forgot about the earthworks near the Observatory and, rushing along in the dark, fell head first into them. Stunned by the fall, he heard a gunshot nearby and was convinced a Yankee had shot him. He found himself unhurt, however, and was overjoyed to discover several cadets left behind on campus (most had already retreated with President Garland) with orders to blow up the powder magazine. These cadets had also heard the gunshot, and they, like Cowan, were convinced that the Yankees had arrived. After a hasty consultation, they decided to forget about blowing up the powder and beat a hasty retreat. Cowan recalled that later he discovered that the gunshot "which had frightened me almost out of my wits and so alarmed the detachment that they had failed to blow up the magazine" had come from his own rifle. It had discharged when he fell into the fortifications.

These earthworks remained a part of the campus landscape until at least 1906, for they appeared prominently on the Greater University Plan (see fig. 13). In later years their significance was forgotten, and they were destroyed.

7 MARR'S SPRING

Marr's Spring served as the university's principal water supply throughout the nineteenth century and well into the twentieth. Water from this source was collected in brick cisterns from which university slaves hauled buckets to the rooms of students. Complete baths were a rarity. They consisted mostly of a swim in the spring or in the nearby Black Warrior River. A bathhouse was constructed near Marr's Spring as early as the 1840s, but by the mid-1880s it was in disrepair. In 1888 a steam-driven pump located in the Pump House and Cadet Laundry [17] was used to pump spring water up the hill to the university buildings. A year later the trustees recorded in their minutes that they were hesitant to repair the bathhouse because "it has always been considered doubtful whether the plunging and swimming in the very cold water so directly from the spring is conducive to health, and often the visit to the bath house is made a pretext for going out of the Military bounds for improper purposes [i.e., going to town]."

In the early twentieth century the branch leading from the spring to the Warrior River was dammed and a new concrete pump house and hydraulic engineering laboratory were erected beside it. The dam has long since been removed, but the pump house now used as a maintenance building is still there. In 1936 water from the spring was backed up by yet another dam to create a swimming lake that became a popular summer recreational area for several generations of university students. The two-year project, a "wheelbarrow, pick and shovel job" done entirely by student labor, provided much-needed jobs for about 650 students. Money was provided by the PWA, which also helped to fund the bathhouse and diving platform. In 2010 the swimming lake that for years had served as a holding pond associated with the heating and cooling plant was converted into an ornamental lake, the spring itself was cleared of debris, the antebellum cisterns refurbished, and the whole area turned into an attractive pocket park. It is interesting to note that the area was sodded with grass salvaged from Bryant-Denny Stadium [103].

8 GORGAS HOUSE

Today the Gorgas House is a museum, but it has an interesting history in its own right. Designed to serve as the "hotel" or "steward's hall," it is the only structure on the campus that has survived from William Nichols's original

(1828) master plan. The ground floor, once paved in brick, originally consisted of one large dining room capable of seating about one hundred students. Behind it were two rooms used as pantries, and the upstairs was the home of the steward and his family. A separate, two-story brick kitchen stood behind the house where Morgan Hall [19] now stands.

Nichols's original plan called for an identical steward's hall to be built on the eastern side of the campus, but the one dining hall proved so difficult to administer that after about fifteen years students were encouraged to board in off-campus private homes.

In the late 1840s the Steward's Hall was remodeled as a faculty residence. In 1853 cast-iron railings for the front steps were ordered from the Cornell Company Iron Works in New York. (Railings for the President's Mansion [4] were ordered at the same time.) The present portico was added in 1895 to provide Mrs. Gorgas with a "piazza," or sitting porch. The original small porch was extended one bay on either side and the stone steps and iron railings were replaced. Although the upper floor was used as a residence, the university reserved the right to use the ground floor for student recitations. One of the last classes held at the university before it was destroyed was held

Gorgas House

here on the fateful afternoon of April 3, 1865. Cowan, whose misadventures in the student fortifications have already been recorded, recalled that his two o'clock class in oratory and rhetoric met at Professor John Wood Pratt's house (Gorgas House) in the recitation room (probably the old dining room downstairs). The excitement generated by rumors of an impending Yankee invasion had kept all the cadets from learning that day's lessons. Recognizing the futility of trying to hold a regular class, Pratt allowed the students to spend the recitation hour discussing the situation. Cowan noted that when "the drum sounded the hour of 3 o'clock, the classes filed out, and very few if any of us ever saw the beloved professor after that hour. Little did he think that the invading foe was then almost in shelling distance of the campus, and but a few hours would elapse ere the doom of the University would be sealed."

In 1879 the house became associated with the Gorgas family. In that year General Josiah Gorgas, the former Confederate chief of ordinance and seventh president of the University of Alabama, resigned because of poor health. Although he had served for only one year, the board of trustees accepted his resignation and, to ease his financial situation, awarded him the post of librarian and assigned the "Pratt House" rent free for his use. Simultaneously, his wife, Amelia Gayle Gorgas, accepted the position of matron of the University Infirmary and postmistress. Both the post office and the infirmary were thereafter in her home.

After General Gorgas's death in 1883 his wife assumed the position of librarian and continued to live in the house until her death in 1913. Her daughters remained in the home, now referred to as the "Gorgas House," until the death of Maria Gorgas, the last surviving child, who lived until 1953. In 1944 the state legislature designated the house a memorial to the Gorgas family but allowed the Gorgas sisters to remain. Today, it contains a wealth of furniture, silver, clothing, and other memorabilia associated with the family. It is open to the public.

9 GUARD HOUSE

The earliest building to reflect the university's new 1860 military form of governance was the Guard House, an essay in crenellated Gothic Revival architecture. It was the first structure to depart from the Classical Revival style William Nichols instituted. In all probability it was the creation of Colonel James T. Murfee, who, like a number of Garland's new faculty, had been trained at the Virginia Military Institute. The neo-Gothic buildings on that campus, designed by Alexander Jackson Davis in the late 1840s, set the architectural style for many military schools and served as the model for later development of the University of Alabama campus.

The Guard House, built in 1862, was intended to shelter cadets on guard duty from inclement weather. Three years later it was also used to house Neil, Gabe, and Crawford, slaves belonging to local citizens, who were hired by the University because of their skills playing the drum and fife.

Perhaps the most historic moment in the life of the Guard House occurred on April 4, 1865. About 12:25 A.M. of that day President Garland received word that Federal troops were crossing the Black Warrior River from Northport and invading Tuscaloosa. He rushed to the Guard House, roused the musicians from their pallets on the floor and ordered them to beat the "long roll" to awake a Cadet Corps allegedly trained for such an emergency. The corps was hurriedly assembled and ordered to march the mile to town to meet the enemy.

But after the cadets' first brief skirmish with General John T. Croxton's 1,400 trained and seasoned soldiers, President Garland decided to withdraw his 300 poorly equipped young boy-soldiers rather than see them slaughtered. The Corps of Cadets hastily retreated back to the university, picked up their haversacks, and hastened down Huntsville Road toward Hurricane Creek.

By late afternoon little remained of the University of Alabama. Only a few faculty residences, the Observatory [5], and the little Guard House were left standing.

When the university reopened in 1871 the university physician used the Guard House as an office. According to one account, malingering cadets would lick the yellow paint on the exterior of the building to coat their tongues before entering to be examined by the doctor. Two years later the Guard House was appropriated for the use of nonmilitary students, who for the first time since 1860 were allowed to enter the institution. In 1888 it was in such a dilapidated condition that some people believed it should be demolished. The trustees noted that "it seemed akin to an act of vandalism to destroy this connecting link between the old and the new." Consequently, they had it repaired and fitted up with a large iron safe to store university records. The Jasons, a men's honor society, was permitted to use it in 1933. In 1990 the antebellum structure was made a memorial site for all university honor societies.

10 CEMETERY

The tour of the antebellum campus ends on a melancholy note with a visit to the university cemetery. In an era of poor transportation and a high mortality rate, institutional graveyards were a necessity. The board of trustees did not concern itself with this problem until Samuel James, a student, died in 1839 and was buried on campus. In their December 16 meeting that year the board passed an ordinance establishing a "burying ground at the university" that was not to exceed one acre and was to include Samuel James's grave. A sum of $100 was appropriated to enclose the cemetery. James's family later disinterred the body, but another student, William J. Crawford, who died of typhus fever on July 6, 1844, was buried in the same grave. President Manly also recorded the burial of two slaves in the cemetery—Jack, a slave belonging to the university, died of "bilious Pneumonia" and was buried there

Guard House

Guard House, ca. 1890

on May 5, 1843. The other was William or "Boysey," a seven-year-old boy Dr. Manly owned, who died of whooping cough on November 22, 1844.

Isolated on the northeastern edge of campus adjacent to a cotton plantation (later the site of Bryce Hospital) owned by Colonel Robert Ellyson, the lonely cemetery soon gave rise to the belief that that area of campus was haunted. It was rumored that Ellyson's slaves refused to go near the college graveyard at night because they had seen strange lights and even a hovering tall white figure. The campus building closest to the cemetery was Jefferson Hall, which, before the construction of Madison Hall, in 1859, stood alone on the east side of campus. It was inhabited mainly by freshmen and sophomores. The "cemetery ghost" was particularly feared by the residents of this dormitory because the student buried there had died in his room in Jefferson Hall.

Later a portion of the burying ground became the property of the Pratt family. Horace S. Pratt, a former professor, died in Georgia and was buried in that state, but members of his family continued to live in Tuscaloosa near the campus and were interred in the university cemetery. In 1854 Mrs. Pratt asked the board of trustees to give her title to that portion of the cemetery in which her relatives were buried. The four tombstones enclosed by the ornate iron fence all mark the graves of members of the Pratt family. In 2004 a marker was placed nearby to memorialize the unlocated graves of university student William Crawford and the slaves William "Boysey" Brown and Jack Rudolph. (The surnames "Brown" and "Rudolph" appearing on the marker were the names of prior owners of these slaves.)

Cemetery

VICTORIAN CAMPUS TOUR

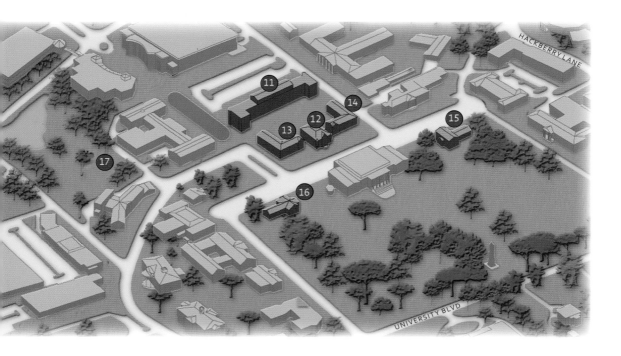

11   Woods Hall

12   Clark Hall

13   Manly Hall

14   Garland Hall

15   Tuomey Hall

16   Oliver-Barnard Hall

17   Pump House and Cadet Laundry (Demolished)

11 WOODS HALL

Woods Hall was the first structure to be built at the university after the close of the Civil War that left most of the campus in ruins. Only the northern half of Colonel James T. Murfee's proposed huge new building was constructed between 1867 and 1868. (See "The Victorian Campus, 1865–1906," p. 7). This section was referred to by everyone as the "barracks" until 1884, at which time it was named Alva Woods Hall in honor of the university's first president.

Murfee described the advantages of the new building in glowing terms in a pamphlet, "A New Scheme of Organization, Institution, and Government for the University of Alabama, With Report on Construction of Building," that he wrote in 1867 to present to the board of trustees. "The style of the architecture is Tudor Gothic, and is consistent with the principles of a refined taste in every detail," he said. "It is particularly expressive for a military establishment, and may be highly esteemed for a civil college. The buttresses, which are one of the prominent features, contribute much to ornament, and, allowing walls of much less thickness, reduce the cost very materially." The galleries on all floors were to serve as the "only pass ways between rooms," and they would also function in inclement weather as "valuable promenades for exercise."

A hardened disciplinarian, Murfee carefully determined the function of each floor and each room to maximize control over students. "When lodged on the first floor, young men are less healthy," he explained. "They are disturbed by hucksters and by idle fellows from the outside; and, at night, they escape through the windows for improper purposes." To avoid such problems the lower floor was to be used for classrooms, society halls, the dining room, and other public rooms. "The students are all above the ground floor, where they are healthfully, comfortably, and quietly situated." Even in their own rooms, however, students were not to be free from supervision. The glass transoms and glazed doors would reveal their activities. "Noise will be heard through the open transoms; lights at improper hours will show through the glass; and an officer on the colonnade can discover any improprieties."

Mindful of the poverty of the state, Murfee was careful to point out that no funds were to be "expended for mere ornament, but a handsome appearance is produced by good proportions, and the relief of light and shade. The beauty of fitness is found in every arrangement; and there is, in all the work of this building for young men, a masculine expression of neatness, simplicity and strength.—The moldings are well relieved, and all the curves are bold."

In March 1867 George M. Figh and Company of Montgomery received the construction contract and agreed to complete the central part of the building by January 1, 1868, and the wings by the following June.

Excavations for the enormous crypt-like cellars under the barracks began at once, but delays brought about by lack of bricks, bad weather, and broken machinery caused construction to take much longer than predicted. Many of the bricks came from the ruins of Washington Hall, but so many were broken that Murfee changed the building specifications to read "American bond" rather than "Flemish bond" in order to use more of the broken "bats." Nevertheless, Murfee needed many thousands of new bricks. These were made only a few hundred yards from the construction site. Unused bats from the ruins were sold to the nearby Alabama Insane Hospital (Bryce) [74], and the special wedge-shaped bricks from the thirty large Ionic columns of the Rotunda and Lyceum were sold to townspeople for wells. The handsome stone column capitals and bases were also sold for use as stepping-stones and garden ornaments. Even after being thoroughly gleaned for salvageable material, huge piles of debris still remained on the sites of the ruined buildings.

As work on Woods Hall continued, the university became enmeshed in corrupt Reconstruction politics. The new Alabama Constitution took control of the school away from the trustees and gave it to an elected state "board of regents." For the next eight years the institution was subject to the worst excesses of the political spoils system. Despite these difficulties, Woods Hall was completed in July 1868. It could house 180 students on its upper floors and feed up to 500 in its huge first-floor dining room. Few students showed up the first year, however, and it was not until the mid-1870s that enrollment began to increase.

The most decorative features of the new building were the cast-iron columns and the hundreds of feet of railings that protected its four long wooden porches, or "stoops," as the students called them. The railings were a combination of cast and wrought iron, created by a process that had been patented in the early 1850s by J. B. Wickersham of the New York Wire Railing Company. They were made of wrought-iron wire, looped and interwoven and set within wrought-iron panels with cast-iron rosette clamps at the crossing of the wires. The result was lighter and less expensive than conventional iron railings. (In 1975, as Woods Hall was being remodeled, many of the railings were found to have lost their decorative rosettes. New ones were cast and attached, and the railings were raised to meet safety codes. At

the same time the original wooden floors of the porches were replaced with fireproof concrete and steel.)

Woods Hall

The central section of the ground floor was used as the main university dining hall for about fifty years. Early twentieth-century alumni recalled its being a hazing ground for freshmen, who were required by upperclassmen to eat their meals in a stooped position (known as "sitting on infinity"). Indeed, the building was a rowdy, raucous place, particularly during football season when whole tables of students tried to out-cheer one another in support of their favorite teams. One old alumnus recounted that "the usual sequel to such demonstrations was a sudden dousing of the lights, followed by the splattering of water or syrup. The only place of escape was under chairs or tables. When the lights were turned back on, the hall looked empty, all of the students having found refuge under the furniture."

The dining hall was the scene of many student dances, or "hops," held during the Christmas holidays and particularly at commencements. It is said that dancing was frowned upon by many local religious denominations whose members regarded it as wicked "night revelry," but university administrators took a more liberal view of the matter and allowed this popular activity to continue.

The towers at each end of the north side of the building were professors' offices that opened into lecture rooms. Their upper stories (once crowned with battlements like the rest of the structure) were obviously planned as guardhouses for sentries. There is no record of their being used for this purpose, however. In fact, in the late 1880s the western tower was reinforced and made into the base for a large water tank (see fig. 10). According to Colonel Murfee's original scheme, the fourth floor was to be used as a cadet hospital. His reasoning was that the elevated location was healthful and isolated, and students who were not really sick would have greater difficulty escaping from their beds undetected. However, the hospital was located elsewhere and the upper stories of Woods Hall were used primarily for dormitories.

Woods Hall underwent its first major renovation in 1909. The April 21, 1909, *Crimson-White* enthusiastically declared, "Old Woods Hall to be Beautiful Dormitory." In that year much of its interior was redesigned by architect Frank Lockwood: fireplaces were sealed off in preparation for the installation of steam heating, and plans were made to paint the entire exterior of the building yellow to match newer campus structures. Despite its renovations, Woods Hall remained quite Spartan in its accoutrements. Married students who lived there during the summers of the 1920s recalled the primitive conditions and the bedbugs. Maintenance workers sprayed daily in a vain attempt to rid the dormitory of these pests.

As one might expect from such an old structure, numerous stories and legends are associated with Woods Hall. If any portion of the Victorian campus is haunted, it must surely be the second floor "stoop" of the barracks. In February 1878 the east end of the porch was the scene of a sensational murder. For years students had been prohibited from carrying weapons. New students were required to sign pledges that they would not have in their possession "a pistol, bowie knife, sword-cane, or any other deadly weapon, except such arms as are furnished by the military department." These pledges appear to have been generally ignored. Cadet Kibble J. Harrison shot and killed Cadet William W. Alston during a quarrel that began over "certain defamatory remarks" Harrison had allegedly made about Alston's cousin. The February 27, 1878, *Tuscaloosa Times* reported that the shooting was the result of "secret societies" (fraternities) that had divided the students into factions. Harrison was arrested on a charge of voluntary manslaughter. A year later a jury found him not guilty.

Today Woods Hall is home to many of the studio spaces of the Department of Art and Art History.

12 CLARK HALL

The center building of the postbellum Quadrangle, named for Willis G. Clark, president of the board of trustees, was the most ornate of three new buildings constructed by New Orleans architect William A. Freret. Ground was broken for it on February 20, 1884, but work progressed slowly because workmen cutting into the cellar of the old Lyceum ruins (see fig. 8) had to dig deeper than anticipated and use more locally made brick than expected. Delays in construction were also caused by the fact that separate contracts were awarded for the brickwork, stonework, carpentry, ironwork, roofing, and painting. Contractors ranged as far afield as Atlanta, Montgomery, Mobile, New Orleans, and Louisville. In the long run this scheme did not save money or prove successful. Unavoidable delays in shipment or production of materials by one contractor hindered the work of the others.

Despite such setbacks the cornerstone of Clark Hall was laid with great ceremony on May 5, 1884, the fifty-second anniversary of the laying of the cornerstone of Franklin Hall [3]. Among the sixteen items placed in it was a silver dime, dated 1821, from the cornerstone of the antebellum dormitory. Many people have been confused about the date of the construction of Clark Hall because of the various dates carved on the stone caps of the lower buttresses on the west side of the building. These dates commemorate later graduating classes, as does the "1901" inscribed on the marble slab in the pavement before the south entrance. The May 28, 1907, *Montgomery Advertiser* recorded that on Class Day the seniors planted the "class ivy"—a custom that had begun two years earlier. "And above each bit of ivy slowly climbing the walls of Clark Hall there is cut in the stone the figures of 1905 and 1906. In cap and gown, the Seniors of 1907 marched out and planted the sprig of ivy which is to be a memorial for the class which today begins the real work of life."

Throughout the remainder of 1884 and during 1885, Clark Hall slowly rose phoenixlike from the site of the old Lyceum. Its facade is dominated by its two large corner towers, which are supported by cast-iron Gothic columns. At one stage of the design these towers were intended as stair towers, but the idea was abandoned as impractical. Freret made extensive use of iron and glass throughout the structure, and its roof bristled with iron roof-cresting. He had utilized a number of the most distinctive decorative

Clark Hall

features, including the corner towers, mansard roof, and iron roof-cresting, from his earlier almshouse and public school commissions in New Orleans. Here, on the university structure, they assumed a grander scale and were more dramatically emphasized.

The interior of Clark Hall has been completely changed. The lower floor was originally intended to house the University Library on the west side and the "winter" chapel on the east. (This later became a part of the library and was used to house its collection of government documents.) The second floor contained the commencement hall, which seated about six hundred people. Two hundred more could be seated in the galleries surrounding it on three sides. On the north side of the large room was an elevated stage, above which were two oculi, or circular windows. Even today, broken into smaller compartments, the interior is awesome in scale. Unfortunately, its acoustics were terrible from the beginning, and the glare from the extremely tall windows was painful. Various remedies were tried to improve the acoustics, and in 1892 the university determined to install wooden blinds to cut down the glare. A sales representative from the Meridian Sash and Blind Company told the trustees that "inside blinds had been going out of style and are now rarely seen in modern public halls devoted to citizens in academic uses." He then persuaded them that the most modern and effective solution to the problem would be the installation of "cathedral glass" in all the windows of the auditorium. ("Cathedral glass" was apparently the trade name for a type of mass-produced, textured, colored glass.) Its roughness of surface, the salesman claimed, would also improve the acoustics of the hall. The trustees liked the idea, and by commencement the auditorium was aglow with a motley of pastel shades of yellow, green, blue, orange, and brown. Cathedral glass proved exceptionally brittle, and the windows were severely damaged a few years later in a hailstorm. As the years passed and the glass broke, it was replaced once again with clear panes. The last remnants of "cathedral glass" were removed in 1948 when the building was renovated. Today it is still possible to find shards of colored glass at the roots of the shrubbery surrounding the building.

The auditorium lost its original function as the school's commencement hall with the completion of Morgan Hall [19] in 1911. In 1928 it was used as a basketball court and "amusement hall" for dances, and for a time before Bidgood Hall [44] was built, housed the School of Commerce and Business Administration. The University Library remained downstairs until 1925 when the first Amelia Gayle Gorgas Library (now Carmichael Hall [43]) was constructed. Declared structurally unsound as early as 1910, Clark Hall, disguised under an all-enveloping coat of yellow paint in 1913, began to look decidedly shabby. By 1948 it was near collapse. The massive roof had caused the outer walls to bulge alarmingly, and extensive interior damage resulted from many leaks. Fred Maxwell, university consulting engineer, working with Ed McCowan of the architectural firm of Miller, Martin, and Lewis, saved the building by erecting an interior steel frame to support the weight of the roof. It was then possible to pull the no-longer-weight-bearing walls back into proper alignment. At this time the auditorium was dismantled and the galleries were extended to form a complete third floor. Ironically, Clark Hall, which for years had been considered unsafe, was now one of the soundest buildings on campus. Civil Defense authorities designated it as a shelter in case of nuclear attack, and boxes and barrels of food and water were stored in the gigantic attic under the mansard roof.

Today Clark Hall houses on the first two floors the offices of the Dean of the College of Arts and Sciences and his staff. The third floor (once the balcony of the old auditorium) is now used as a studio by the Department of Theatre and Dance.

Above: Manly Hall (foreground) and Woods Hall (background), ca. 1890

Right: Manly Hall

13 MANLY HALL

Manly Hall, erected in 1884 at the same time as Clark Hall [12], was named after the second president of the university, the Reverend Basil Manly. It is located on the site of one of the original 1828 faculty duplexes and recitation rooms. In 1981 excavations for the installation of an elevator in Manly Hall uncovered portions of the foundations of one of these early dwellings and the base of a chimney. Manly Hall was designed to contain much-needed dormitories and classrooms as well as the president's office, which was located for many years on the ground floor. The main classroom for the Law

School was also located there just inside the south entrance. This entrance retains its original configuration, while that of Garland Hall [14] has been radically changed. Manly and Garland halls were once decorated with a vibrant display of Victorian finery, including common and pressed brick, terra cotta panels along the cornice, iron roof-cresting, dormer windows in the roof, and large, two-story, traceried windows in the end gables. The roof-cresting and dormer windows were removed in 1902. It is to be hoped that someday they will be replaced.

A few years later in 1913 the vivid Victorian polychromy, so prized in the 1880s and so despised during the first half of the twentieth century, was further obscured when all the buildings of the Victorian campus were painted yellow in an attempt to tone them down and blend them with the new campus buildings. The paint, and, alas, much of the finish of the bricks, was finally removed in 1948 when the buildings were sandblasted.

Manly Hall is now the home of the departments of Religious Studies and Women's Studies.

14 GARLAND HALL

Not wishing to repeat the mistakes it had made in the erection of Clark [12] and Manly [13] halls, the board of trustees awarded the entire contract for Garland Hall (named after the university's third president, Landon Cabell Garland) to one Mobile contractor. He was allowed to use the bricks left over from the other buildings, but problems arose because there were not enough of them, and it was too wet to make more locally. He tried to buy bricks elsewhere but discovered that they did not harmonize with those made of Tuscaloosa clay. He had to resort to making bricks in the Insane Hospital kilns, with the result that Garland Hall was not completed for many months. Garland Hall was finally handed over to the university in March 1888.

The board of trustees appropriated the third floor of the new building for its own use and furnished it. The committee reported in June 1888 that "although the appointments and conveniences of the Trustees' rooms may not equal the comforts of home they are sufficiently removed from asceticism or parsimony (which the state does not expect or require of its unpaid servants) to make them inhabitable and attractive enough to prevent anxiety on the part of occupants to get away before their official work is completed."

The second floor housed members of the senior class because it was felt that they would take better care of the new building and would be less likely to disturb the trustees above them.

Garland Hall

The ground floor was used for the Natural History Museum and the offices of its director, Professor Eugene Allen Smith. Largely due to Smith, the collection had grown dramatically since 1873. It had heretofore been kept in the basement of Woods Hall. Now, with advice from experts at the Smithsonian Institution, it was possible to display it properly. The museum remained in the building until the completion of Smith Hall in 1911. After serving a variety of purposes through the years, the old museum was converted in 1967 into an art gallery. The Sarah Moody Gallery under the direction of the Department of Art and Art History is open to the public throughout the year for faculty, student, and traveling exhibitions. The rest of the building houses art history offices and classrooms on the second and third floors.

15 TUOMEY HALL

While work on the last of William A. Freret's three buildings was still going on, the board of trustees determined to construct two additional structures. After consulting with several Montgomery architects, the board chose W. A. Crossland's plan for the design of a laboratory for the Department of Chemistry to be named after professor and state geologist Michael Tuomey. Crossland designed a successful blending of this building and the slightly later, but almost identical Barnard (now Oliver-Barnard) Hall [16] with

Above: Tuomey Hall

Left: Tuomey Hall, ca. 1890s

Freret's earlier structures. He used similar materials and devices, including terra cotta plaques, iron roof ornaments, and decorative brickwork. The building contained chemistry laboratories, classrooms, and the offices of the Alabama Geological Survey. The scientific apparatus from the early chemistry department is on permanent display in the W. S. Hoole Special Collections Library.

Tuomey lost its original function with the erection of later and larger buildings. From 1926 to 1999 the Army Reserve Officers Training Corps (ROTC) used it for their offices and classrooms. In 2000 Tuomey and Barnard halls were renovated by the Blount Undergraduate Initiative program as "academic houses" for upperclassmen in the program. Freshmen Blount scholars are required to live in the Blount Living-Learning Center [69].

16 OLIVER-BARNARD HALL

Barnard Hall, completed in 1889, was designed as a physical laboratory and gymnasium and named after Frederick A. P. Barnard, antebellum professor and scientist. The two-story section housed the astronomy classroom and engineering departments. The board of trustees had originally intended to erect a new observatory as part of this building, but upon investigation they determined that the original location was preferable and that the old building (now Maxwell Hall [5]) would be too costly to replace. When Comer Hall [18] was completed the Department of Physics and Astronomy and the Department of Engineering were moved out of Barnard Hall and replaced by the School of Law. This school, in turn, later moved to new quarters on the third floor of Morgan Hall [19] in 1911. In later years Barnard Hall housed the Air Force ROTC program until 1999 when it, like Tuomey Hall [15], was remodeled by the Blount Undergraduate Initiative. At that time it was renamed Oliver-Barnard Hall to honor John T. Oliver, a Jasper businessman and university trustee emeritus.

The west wing of Barnard Hall contained the student gymnasium—the first of its kind in the state and one of the first in the region. Its construction reflected the growing interest in sports on American college campuses in the last quarter of the nineteenth century. The Building Committee recorded that "as there were no experts capable of advising in the matter here, and the committee desired the fullest information before acting, they entered into correspondence with Dr. Adams of Johns Hopkins University who recommended Professor Crenshaw in charge of the Gymnasium of Randolph Macon College, Virginia." Professor Crenshaw traveled to Tuscaloosa, met with the committee, and assisted in drawing plans and writing specifications for this project. He agreed to return to the university in May 1889 "to superintend putting up the apparatus and organize and instruct a class for exhibition during commencement week." The university hired his assistant, Marcellus T. Hayes, as the first director and instructor in the gymnasium.

The Victorian era saw the advent of team sports as well. Baseball had become popular on campus as early as the mid-1870s. (In the antebellum period Professor Tuomey had attempted to interest students in the English game of cricket with little success.) Football, which eventually eclipsed all

Oliver-Barnard Hall

Barnard Hall, ca. 1890s

the other team sports in popularity, was introduced in 1892. The gymnasium in Barnard Hall was used until the completion of Little Hall [23a] in 1915.

Barnard Hall and the other campus structures were illuminated by electricity in 1888, but power outages were common because university cadets soon discovered the dramatic (and shocking) effects resulting from sticking their bayonets in the light sockets.

17 Pump House and Cadet Laundry (Demolished)

The small brick building once located directly behind Comer Hall [18] was constructed in 1888 as part of the university's waterworks. It contained steam-powered machinery for pumping water from Marr's Spring [7] up to tanks on top of one of the towers of Woods Hall [11] and in the attic of Garland Hall [14], which provided running water for the first time in the university's history. Before the construction of this building, water was obtained from Marr's Spring and from wells located beside many of the campus buildings (the only surviving one is located behind the Gorgas House [8]). "Stoop boys" (university slaves in the antebellum period and hired servants after the war) carried buckets of water to dormitory rooms so that students could perform their ablutions.

The pump house also contained the cadet laundry. The abundance of hot water and steam was used to wash and iron the cadets' uniforms based on those worn at West Point. According to the 1894 *Corolla*, "Every Monday morning the wagon goes round and gathers up the clothes bags which the cadets have thrown over the stoops. We get them back Saturday morning." There was even a specialized machine for pressing cadet collars.

Electricity was also generated in the pump house—enough to "light up the stoops" with every room containing a 16- or 32-watt incandescent light.

The Pump House and Cadet Laundry photographed before its demolition in July 2012.

When the engineering building, Comer Hall [18], was built in front of it, the building was converted into a foundry and blacksmith shop for the department of mechanical engineering. In recent years theater students used its upper floor for the construction of sets and storage, and art students used the lower floor for studios. This sturdy 124-year-old structure was the last remaining service building from the Victorian-era campus when it was razed in 2012.

Laundry workers, ca 1890. Note the roof of the old bathhouse at Marr's Spring in the background.

TOUR 3

EARLY TWENTIETH-CENTURY CAMPUS TOUR

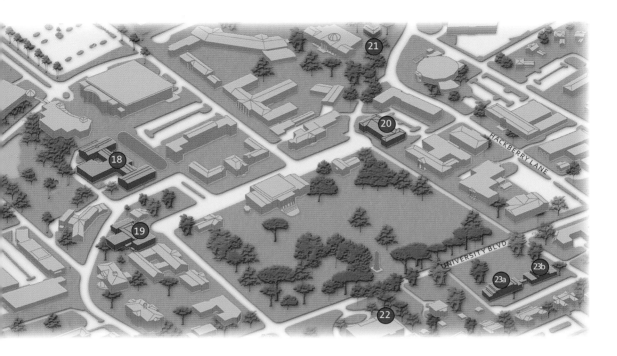

18	Comer Hall
19	Morgan Hall
20	Smith Hall
21	Kilgore House
22	Tutwiler Hall (Demolished)
23a	Little Hall
23b	Moore Hall

18 COMER HALL

Montgomery architect Frank Lockwood designed Comer Hall, the first of the Greater University buildings to be completed. It was named in honor of Alabama Governor Braxton Bragg Comer who, as a university cadet in 1865, had experienced firsthand the destruction of his alma mater. (See "The Greater University Plan, 1906," p. 13.) Albert Chadwick, one of Lockwood's associates, actually supervised its construction and that of Smith Hall [20]. Both were erected between 1907 and 1910. Comer Hall opened in April 1909 and the following winter the new power plant located in its west wing provided steam heat for campus buildings. Over a century later the building continues to house the central power plant. For years its gigantic red smokestack, erected in 1967, dominated the skyline of the campus and was the inspiration for many campus jokes. No longer needed, it was removed in 2010.

Designed for use by the School of Engineering, Comer Hall was in its day one of the finest buildings of its type in the South. The School of Engineering had only recently been created, but the university had been one of the first institutions in the country to teach the subject. (Engineering courses had been added to the curriculum in 1837.) The exterior of Comer Hall, unlike the other campus buildings of that era, does not have a colonnade. Instead, it features a continuous two-story blind arcade of segmental arches inset with tripartite sash windows on both floors. Roundels of stone between the   Comer Hall

arcade arches, massive triangular pediments above the doors, and a denticulated cornice below the low mansard roof add interest to this massive, masculine, and rather austere edifice.

After his term as governor, Comer continued to be interested in his namesake. At his death in 1927 he left the Engineering School three of his prized possessions: stuffed trophy heads of a wild mountain goat and a caribou that he had shot on a hunting trip in British Columbia, and a large oil portrait of himself. For many years this odd trio of objects was prominently displayed in the dean's office in Comer Hall.

Comer Hall is now home to the Department of Modern Languages and Classics and the Language Resource Center.

19 MORGAN HALL

The exterior of Morgan Hall, designed by Frank Lockwood and completed in 1911, is almost identical to that of Smith Hall [20], toward which it faces. The building consists of a three-story central block containing classrooms and offices in the front and a large auditorium in the rear. On each side are smaller wings containing more classrooms, offices, and stairs. The building was named after Senator John Tyler Morgan, who in 1882 had helped to obtain the indemnity from the federal government for the destruction of the University of Alabama campus in 1865.

Morgan Hall

Morgan Hall, like Comer [18] and Smith [20] halls, was built of Missouri

yellow brick, with stone trim. These materials met with opposition from an unexpected source. The Manufacturers Association of Alabama objected to the use of Missouri brick and adopted a resolution in May 1908 requesting that preference be given to "materials and supplies of Alabama manufacture for all purchases made for and in behalf of the state." The next buildings constructed on campus, Tutwiler [22] and Little [23a] halls, were built of Alabama red brick.

Morgan Hall now houses the Department of English. Its handsome and ornate auditorium is used for fiction and poetry readings and dance performances.

Several of the magnolia trees in front of Morgan Hall were planted in 1910 by Mrs. Netta Tutwiler McCorvey, the wife of a history professor and the daughter of Henry Tutwiler, one of the university's original faculty members. Mrs. McCorvey was distressed by the lack of landscaping around the new building, so she transplanted magnolia seedlings from her residence located on the site of Little Hall [23a]. The parent tree was a large magnolia that once grew between the McCorvey house and the President's Mansion [4].

20 SMITH HALL

Smith Hall, at the opposite end of Capstone Drive, was named after university professor Eugene Allen Smith, who had been appointed state geologist in 1873. Dr. Smith spent nearly forty years surveying, mapping, and collecting scientific specimens throughout the state.

Like Comer [18] and Morgan [19] halls, Smith Hall, designed by Frank Lockwood, was constructed of gray Bedford stone from Indiana and yellow brick from Missouri. It consists of a three-story central section for the University Natural History Museum. On the north is a two-story wing that originally housed the Department of Biology. To the south a matching wing contained geology classrooms and offices. The building, designed in the Classical Revival style, features in the center an engaged colonnade of eight Ionic columns raised above a full basement. The main entrance at ground level is through a massive pedimented stone doorway. On the interior is a spacious center hall dominated by a sweeping Alabama marble and Alabama-manufactured iron staircase leading to the museum above. The newel posts contain cartouches with "U of A" inscribed in the center.

The architecture of the museum reflected, on a more modest scale, the design and layout of the great natural history museums only recently constructed in Chicago, New York, and Washington, DC. The main display area

Smith Hall

on the second floor is surrounded by a colonnade of Corinthian columns that supports a full entablature with a highly enriched cornice. Spanning the colonnade is a large glass roof that floods the interior with light. Exhibits are housed in glass and polished wood cases on the second floor and along the ample third-floor mezzanine between the columns. Despite the fact that it is not particularly well adapted to current ideas about museum display, the big sunlit room is one of the most beautifully proportioned interiors on campus.

The university has had a natural history museum since its opening in 1831. A week before school opened on April 6, 1831, the *Alabama State Intelligencer* informed Tuscaloosans that the museum's curator had just returned from Mobile with an "interesting collection of sea-fowls, fishes and shells." The stuffed birds included pelicans, terns, gulls, sea mews, canvas back ducks, American widgeons, and buffleheads. He also brought back a live South American coatimundi, which must have fascinated university students.

The most important antebellum collections were amassed by Professor Michael Tuomey, who was hired as professor of mineralogy and geography while he served as first state geologist. Most of Tuomey's collections, however, were destroyed by the fire of 1865. Those specimens escaping destruction lost much of their scientific value by the loss of their labels during the turbulent Reconstruction period between 1865 and 1873. The present collections date from 1873 when Professor Eugene Allen Smith was appointed director of the State Geological Survey. These now range in the millions of specimens and represent a major survey of Alabama's natural heritage. The museum is open to the public throughout the year.

Some of the university's larger geological specimens, found at various Alabama sites, are permanently displayed in front of the museum. To the left of the main entrance is a rectangular stone slab, bearing ripple marks formed by the action of water in an ancient sea, now preserved forever in sandstone. To its right, nearest the building, is a fossil tree trunk, a *Lepidodendron,* or scale tree, from the coal measures of north Alabama. In front is a chunk of Red Mountain hematite, or red iron ore, the basis of Birmingham's iron industry. To the right of the entrance (nearest the building) is another fossil tree trunk, a *Sigillaria*. In front is a geode of limonite, or brown iron ore, a type found scattered throughout Alabama. This iron ore formed the basis for the Civil War iron industry in the state. The slab of rock to the south of these fossils is a section of fossilized seashore showing mud cracks.

21 KILGORE HOUSE

The Kilgore House, located on what was then the western edge of the Bryce Hospital campus, is a Queen Anne style frame house built in 1890 that played an important role in coeducation at the Capstone. Julia Strudwick Tutwiler, daughter of one of the university's original faculty members, and a noted educator and advocate of women's rights, succeeded in opening the university's doors to women in 1893. However, it was not until 1898, again at her insistence, that coeds were allowed to live on campus. In that year a former faculty house located on the present site of Bibb Graves Hall [41] became the first women's dormitory (then called a "Ranch"). Many women continued to room and board in nearby private homes such as that of Captain C. C. Kilgore, engineer of Bryce Hospital. Mrs. Kilgore made extra money by renting rooms to students. Between 1905 and 1908 sixteen coeds lived at the "Kilgore Ranch," which also served as the home of the university's first female faculty member, Anna Hunter (BS 1903, MS 1904) who roomed there.

Early university coeds (and female faculty) faced many challenges in this formerly all male institution. Some members of the administration were uncomfortable with the presence of women on campus and attempted to monitor their lives. The elderly Dr. Wyman, acting president in 1901, in a letter advised the fourteen "young ladies" entering school that year that,

Kilgore House

We think it best that you should wear a simple black uniform consisting of the Oxford cap and gown, in all public places, also and especially when attending classes. The purchasing of these gowns will be some additional expense at first; but in the end will prove to be an economy of time and money, inasmuch as you can wear beneath the gown the simplest and most inexpensive home-dresses. . . . You can wear them, if made of good material, year after year during your college career. . . . You will also be so inconspicuous by all dressing alike, that no one can accuse you of dressing with the view of attracting young men, your fellow students.

He went on to suggest that they not attend "dancing parties, or in fact any social gatherings of both sexes" during their first year at the university. The twentieth century's first coeds ignored Dr. Wyman's stuffy (but well-meant) advice and photographs of the "Kilgore Ranch" girls now housed in the Hoole Special Collections Library depict them in fashionable attire—not academic gowns and "inexpensive homedresses." However, rules concerning dress and social decorum regarding coeds were strictly enforced at the university for the next sixty-five years, as many living alumnae remember.

The university acquired the Kilgore House—the last remaining female "ranch" and only structure left directly related to women's early struggles to gain acceptance at the university—as part of an extensive land swap between the school and Bryce Hospital in 1971. In 1976 the house was placed on the Alabama Register of Historic Places, and the university renovated it for use by the Center for the Study of Southern History and Culture. For a number of years it also housed the offices of the *Alabama Review,* the scholarly journal of the Alabama Historical Association. From 1986 to 2012 the Kilgore House was the home of *Alabama Heritage,* a magazine devoted to the history of the state and region. In 2012 the university, wishing to build a dining hall on the site, declared the historic house "surplus property" and put it up for sale or demolition despite protests from members of the academic community, architectural historians, and preservationists. As this guide goes to press its fate remains uncertain.

22 TUTWILER HALL (DEMOLISHED)

Tutwiler Hall, the last of the four Greater University buildings to be funded by the 1907 act of the legislature, was finally erected in 1914. It bore the name of Julia Strudwick Tutwiler, who succeeded in opening the doors of the university to women in 1893.

Frank Lockwood designed Tutwiler Hall, but it differed from his other buildings in that it consisted of Alabama red brick. Its most distinctive feature was a colossal, hexastyle Tuscan Doric portico. Other decorative elements included inset plaques and keystones enlivening the facade. Tutwiler was enlarged twice during the 1930s as women's enrollment rose, and it formed the nucleus of the "women's campus" developed in the 1920s and 1930s in the southwest section of the campus. The central portion of

Tutwiler Hall was demolished in 1968.

Tutwiler was demolished in 1968 to make way for Rose Administration Building [35], and a new thirteen-story women's residence hall [72], located several blocks to the south on Bryant Drive, was named in Miss Tutwiler's honor.

23 LITTLE HALL AND MOORE HALL

The Society of the Alumni had been thwarted in 1907, during President Abercrombie's tenure, in its attempt to secure state funds for a new gymnasium. Undaunted by this setback the society sought the money elsewhere, and on May 5, 1909, the *Crimson-White* enthusiastically announced that the "Alumni Plan a Whirlwind Campaign to Raise Funds for Immediate Erection of a Great Gymnasium." It was not until 1915, under a new administration led by President George H. Denny, that the alumni and students achieved their goal. The new gymnasium [23a], on the south side of University Boulevard, east of the President's Mansion, was later named Little Hall in honor of William Gray Little, a student from Livingston who had introduced football to the campus in 1892. Little, a transfer student from Phillips-Andover, weighed a muscular 220 pounds. His Alabama teammates were considerably lighter. The 1894 *Corolla* lamented the poor showing of the first two football teams, but it confidently looked to the future. "We live in hope . . . that fortune will favor us and send us a few heavy men next year; for a foot-ball team to win, must have *heavy* men. Our team of '93–'94 was unusually light, averaging only one hundred and forty-seven (147) pounds."

Architect Frank Lockwood elected to let Little Hall form a pendant to Tutwiler Hall [22], completed the year before on the west side of the President's Mansion [4]. The central section contained the gymnasium.

In the interior was a large main hall used for basketball and general exercises with well-designed galleries at either end for spectators. There were also rooms for boxing, wrestling, special exercises, trophies, athletic teams, lockers, baths, and offices. In 1930 a similar gymnasium for women, Barnwell Hall [38], was erected on the "women's campus" facing Bryant Drive. In 1935, Little Hall was enlarged with the addition of a new building to the east designed by the Birmingham architectural firm Miller, Martin, and Lewis. Known simply as the Men's Gym Annex for forty years, it was designated Moore Hall in 1975 to honor A. B. Moore, a university history professor and first dean of the Graduate School. Little Hall now houses the School of Social Work and Moore Hall is the home of the Department of Kinesiology.

Little Hall (right) served as the men's gymnasium for many years, and Moore Hall (left) was built as an annex to the men's gymnasium.

EAST QUAD TOUR

24 Amelia Gayle Gorgas Library

25 ROTC Building (Former US Bureau of Mines)

26 Lloyd Hall

27 Nott Hall

28 Gallalee Hall

29 Russell Hall

30 Nurses' Home

31 Farrah Hall

32 Foster Auditorium, Malone-Hood Plaza, and Lucy Clock Tower

33a Mary Burke Hall

33b Martha Parham Hall

24 AMELIA GAYLE GORGAS LIBRARY

The university's library was named after Amelia Gayle Gorgas, wife of the school's president, General Josiah Gorgas. For a quarter of a century Mrs. Gorgas served as the university's librarian, until she retired at the age of eighty in 1907.

Funds from the PWA made it possible to erect this long-awaited permanent library building. Completed in 1939 the new Amelia Gayle Gorgas Library was designed by Hugh Martin of the Birmingham architectural firm Miller, Martin, and Lewis. Rather than follow the Million Dollar Plan (see fig. 15), which would have necessitated the costly removal of Clark [12], Manly [13], Garland [14], and Woods [11] halls, Martin returned to the older Greater University Plan (see fig. 13), and erected the new library just north of the site of the original Rotunda. It was located in such a way that the great staircase rested exactly upon the northern half of the foundations of the antebellum building. This symbolic placement was emphasized in 1984 with the creation of the Rotunda Plaza [1]. The fact that the original library had been destroyed in the Civil War is said to have played a part in obtaining federal funds to build the 1939 building. President Richard Clark Foster and (then) Chancellor George Denny went to Washington to meet with President Franklin Delano Roosevelt and ask for government funds for the proposed library. The president listened with interest but told his visitors that PWA assistance was available only to libraries that were fire hazards or had been damaged by fire. President Foster and Chancellor Denny quickly assured him that the University Library was indeed a victim of fire, for Federal troops had burned it during the Civil War. Roosevelt appreciated their argument, and the university received the requested funds. About 45 percent of the cost of the building was paid by the PWA.

In 1939 the Gorgas Library was the largest structure on campus. It closes off the view of the old Victorian campus, but while it dominates the northern end of the Quadrangle, it was designed and scaled to harmonize with the older, smaller buildings bordering the Quad. The Ionic colonnade of the central block corresponds in style and scale to the facade of the President's Mansion [4] to the south. The library is approached by a massive stone staircase leading to a spacious lobby, behind which were at first tiers of book stacks. Above the center portion of the exterior is a high stone attic decorated with allegorical bas-relief plaques. This central block is flanked on the east and west by slightly lower gabled wings that originally housed reading rooms.

Amelia Gayle Gorgas
Library

By the 1960s the collection had outgrown the original building, which had been designed with stacks and storage for approximately five hundred thousand volumes. Instead of building a large new library at another location, the old building was enlarged by additional stories and by expanding it in the rear to the edge of Capstone Drive. Although providing much-needed space for the library's growing collections, the new additions designed by Davis, Speake Associates of Birmingham had a serious impact on the visual and functional integrity of not just the library itself but the entire central campus. Typical of the rejection in the 1960s of the idea of a pedestrian Beaux-Arts campus in favor of an automobile-oriented environment, the north addition was intended to be the new "front" entrance to a library that catered to patrons arriving by car. Capstone Drive, originally conceived by Greater University planners as a mall, had, by the close of the twentieth century, become a crowded parking lot. The 2007 Campus Master Plan (see fig. 18) returned the campus to a more pedestrian friendly environment by closing off three of the streets around the Quad to all vehicular traffic except for bicycles and university buses. Anticipated renovations to the library include modifications to the "modern" north facade to make it harmonize with the rest of the building.

25 ROTC Building (Former US Bureau of Mines)

ROTC Building

The university had abandoned its military form of governance in 1903. Thirteen years later, according to the October 8, 1916, *Montgomery Advertiser,* it became the first state school to inaugurate the reserve officers training corps authorized by Congress for nonmilitary schools. The plan called for "one hour a week of class-room work on the theory of military discipline and life and two hours of drill." Students were given one hour of credit and were exempted from compulsory physical education. Eventually the Army and Air Force ROTC programs moved into Tuomey [15] and Barnard [16] halls, where they remained until these buildings were taken over by the Blount Undergraduate Initiative. At that time the ROTC programs were moved across Capstone Drive to the former home of the Bureau of Mines, which it now shares with the College of Arts and Sciences' Office of Educational Technology.

In 1919 the legislature declared the Department of Mining Engineering at the university to be the official "School of Mines" for the state of Alabama. This declaration made it possible for the federal government to establish a regional experiment station of the US Bureau of Mines on the campus, which would serve the entire southeast. Nine of the eleven experiment stations that were eventually built across the country were located at state universities. The rationale was that the stations could take advantage of the educational facilities and also have greater access to state agencies. The experiment station proved successful over the next decade, and in 1936 the Bureau used PWA funds to commission the architectural firm of Miller, Martin, and Lewis to build a large new Classical Revival building featuring a portico with "Tower of the Winds" columns. During World War II the structure was the site of important projects aimed at improving the processing of materials essential to the war effort. The experiment station remained active up to the 1990s. However, in 1994, as part of a government downsizing, the US Bureau of Mines determined to close it and transferred ownership of the building to the university.

26 LLOYD HALL

Chemistry has always been an important part of the curriculum of the university. In the antebellum period it was taught in the Lyceum (now the site of Clark Hall [12]) as a part of "Natural Philosophy." A number of early professors were distinguished in this field, among them Richard T. Brumby, whose experiments with gold plating paralleled those of Michael Faraday, and Frederick A. P. Barnard who in 1849 introduced the nation's first courses in organic chemistry.

Lloyd Hall

By the 1920s chemistry had long since outgrown its cramped quarters in Tuomey Hall [15], and in 1927 a new building was constructed on the east side of the Quadrangle, where the home of the commandants had stood since 1889. The new structure, designed by the Birmingham firm Warren, Knight, and Davis, was named in honor of Stewart J. Lloyd, the first dean of the School of Chemistry, Metallurgy, and Ceramics. Like most of the academic buildings of this period, a projecting central portico of Tuscan Doric columns dominates its facade. An unusual feature is the use of overscale stone quoins at the corners, the stone standing out in sharp contrast to the red brick.

In the 1960s the building was greatly enlarged by an addition to the rear that bears the name of Professor Jack P. Montgomery, who, with Dean Lloyd, was largely responsible for the growth of the study of chemistry at the university in the first half of the twentieth century.

Lloyd Hall was vacated by the Department of Chemistry and in 2009 was converted into a general university classroom building with new classrooms, offices, a computer lab, and food services.

27 NOTT HALL

William Nichols's 1828 plan for the University of Alabama (see fig. 1) set aside the southern side of the campus for the state's medical college, but when the medical school was finally created in 1859, it was located in Mobile, rather than in Tuscaloosa. The Mobile school was discontinued in 1920, and a new two-year medical program was begun on the Tuscaloosa campus.

Nott Hall, named for Dr. Josiah Nott, founder of the medical school, was constructed in 1922 by Miller, Martin, and Lewis. It is raised on a formal, stone basement or ground floor. The main or second story of red brick, reached by a double flight of stone stairs, features a classical portico of four Roman Ionic stone columns. The design of the building, obviously influenced by the President's Mansion [4] and the Gorgas House [8], initiated a general pattern for other structures destined to be erected around the Quadrangle. In the 1920s and 1930s this style was often referred to as "Southern Colonial" or even "Georgian"; today it would be described as a Palladian version of "Classical Revival."

In 1945 the two-year medical program was expanded into a full School of Medicine and moved to Birmingham where better hospital facilities were available.

Nott Hall was used by the Department of Biology for many years until

Nott Hall

the completion of the Biology Building [60] in 1971. Today it is the home of the Honors College.

28 GALLALEE HALL

The area south of Nott Hall, on the corner of University Boulevard, was from 1859 the site of the home of Professor Eugene Allen Smith, one of the few buildings to survive the Federal destruction of the antebellum campus. The house was later modified for other uses and was finally demolished in 1949 to make way for a new physics-astronomy building eventually named after President John M. Gallalee.

By the time Gallalee Hall was constructed (1949) the idea of designing traffic circles at the east and west entrances to campus and constructing buildings with corner entrances had been abandoned. The impracticality of these circles, together with the reaction of many architects in the postwar era to the classical tradition in general and to Beaux-Arts planning in particular, caused their rejection. Although Miller, Martin, and Lewis received the commission for Gallalee Hall, younger architects now working for the firm obviously had a hand in the new designs. Rather than use the traditional combination of a formal basement surmounted by a projecting classical portico reached by steps, they developed a new one that was to become, with variations, the usual formula for university buildings for the next quarter of a century.

Gallalee Hall, with its practical ground-floor side entrances, is essentially a modern, utilitarian building to which has been applied a minimum of stock classical decorative details in a rather halfhearted attempt to "relate" or "harmonize" the structure with the surrounding older campus buildings. Its most interesting feature is the large observatory dome on the roof. The 20-foot-diameter, copper-over-steel dome is rotated by a friction cable driven by an electric motor. Within is a 10-inch refracting telescope supported on a 2-ton mounting.

Gallalee Hall

29 RUSSELL HALL

Russell Hall, designed in 1968 by Birmingham architect Charles McCauley in a Modernist style, and named after university trustee Thomas D. Russell and his wife, Julia, served as the student infirmary until 2006. In 2012, TurnerBatson Architects of Birmingham completely remodeled the building's exterior with a columned portico at the front and an addition to the rear housing a four-hundred-seat lecture hall and four large classrooms.

Student health has always been a concern of university administrators. In the early 1920s President George H. Denny, realizing the benefits of better health care for his students, donated to the city of Tuscaloosa a lot on the university grounds for the construction of Druid City Hospital. This structure, designed by Birmingham architect D. O. Whilldin in 1923 in a Classical Revival style that harmonized with the nearby academic buildings

Russell Hall

Rendering of Russell
Hall Renovation

on the Quad, contained sixty beds. By World War II the hospital was no longer large enough to meet the needs of the city, and in 1946 hospital administrators leased a portion of Northington General Hospital, a temporary army hospital that closed at the end of the war. The 1923 building was taken over by the university, which used it as a student infirmary until 1968 when the present Russell Hall was built directly in front of it. After the construction of the new building, the old hospital was demolished, but its adjoining Nurses' Home [30] still stands.

30 NURSES' HOME

In 1923, even before the new Druid City Hospital was completed, it became evident that additional space would be needed to house nurses for the fa-

Nurses' Home

The Nurses' Home,
ca. 1950. The portico
roof was originally
surmounted by a
handsome balustrade.

cility. A local businessman, J. T. Horne, provided the funds to construct the edifice, and hospital architect D. O. Whilldin designed it at no charge in an attractive Colonial Revival style. The building created a homelike setting for off-duty nurses. According to contemporary accounts the first floor contained living rooms, a reception room, kitchenette, and breakfast room. Nurses ate their main meals in a dining room in the hospital. The second floor contained bedrooms and a large sleeping porch typical of the era.

Druid City Hospital nurses occupied the Nurses' Home for twenty-four years. From 1951 to 1954 it housed the university's School of Nursing—the first state-supported nursing program in Alabama. It was moved to the medical center in Birmingham in 1969. (For information about the later Capstone College of Nursing, see [84].)

31 FARRAH HALL

The university's School of Law was founded in 1872. Before the construction of Farrah Hall in 1927, it was originally located in Woods Hall [11]. In 1910 it was moved to Manly Hall [13]. Simultaneously, the upper floor of Barnard Hall [16] became the Law School Library. When Morgan Hall [19] was completed in 1911, the peripatetic school moved there.

Farrah Hall

Farrah Hall, the Law School's own building at last, was designed by

Miller, Martin, and Lewis to face the never-built traffic circle that was to define the southeastern edge of campus. It is dominated by a dramatic distyle-in-antis Greek Doric corner entrance reached by a high flight of stairs. The building was named after Dean Albert J. Farrah, who, during his thirty-year association with the school, raised the entrance requirements and expanded the study of law into a three-year program.

The Law School moved out of Farrah Hall when the Law Center [92] was completed in 1978, and the old building is now the home of the Department of Criminal Justice and the Department of Geography's Cartography Laboratory and Map Library.

32 FOSTER AUDITORIUM, MALONE-HOOD PLAZA, AND LUCY CLOCK TOWER

Foster Auditorium, completed in 1939, was designed by Miller, Martin, and Lewis as a multipurpose facility with a seating capacity of 5,400. It has been used for graduation exercises, indoor athletic events, concerts, lectures, and other large gatherings including registration.

The advent of the Great Depression slowed the building program during the last years of Denny's administration. But with President Richard Clark Foster's tenure, construction picked up because the university benefited

The front of Foster Auditorium now faces Malone-Hood Plaza, the focal point of which is the Lucy Clock Tower.

from PWA funds. These underwrote Foster Auditorium and several other buildings in the late 1930s. The auditorium was named in honor of President Foster who died in office in 1941.

Foster Auditorium became the center of international attention on Tuesday, June 11, 1963, when Governor George C. Wallace stood in its north entrance to deny two black students the right to enroll at the university. He did not withdraw until that afternoon, when a brigadier general of the Alabama National Guard (federalized by President Kennedy after the first confrontation with the governor) requested that Wallace "step aside" on orders from the president of the United States. The governor then read a statement and left, and two black students, Vivian Malone and James A. Hood enrolled in the institution. This momentous event is commemorated in the Malone Hood Plaza in front of the building. An earlier attempt to integrate the university is commemorated by the clock tower. In 1956 Autherine Lucy became the first African American to attend classes at the Capstone. Public hostility toward her admission and the threat of mob violence caused the board of trustees to suspend her after only two days, however. Despite this setback she earned a graduate degree from the university thirty years later.

Foster Auditorium was declared a National Historic Landmark in 2005. Five years later the building was renovated and expanded to house the women's volleyball and basketball programs. The Birmingham firm of Davis Architects was responsible for the renovations as well as the design for the memorial plaza and clock tower.

33 MARY BURKE AND MARTHA PARHAM HALLS

The first of several large dormitory complexes built during the 1960s, Mary Burke Hall was completed in 1962, just in time to meet the housing needs of the vanguard of the postwar baby boom. It was named for Mary Burke, dean of women from 1921 to 1927. The work of Birmingham architect Lawrence S. Whitten, it was built as two units, each designed to house 262 women.

In 1963 a nearly identical dormitory complex, capable of housing 524 women, was opened across Sixth Avenue on Denny Field. It was named after Martha Parham, who served for many years as registrar and director of women's housing.

Women students were required to live on campus until the early 1970s, and many alumnae remember the strictly enforced curfews regulating the lives of university coeds. Every night the well-lit entrances to Mary Burke

and Martha Parham halls were the scenes of frenzied activity as coeds bolted from countless automobiles to race against time to "sign in." Unfortunate individuals who had lingered too long were disciplined, including a dreaded interview with the dean of women.

Mary Burke Hall and Martha Parham Hall

WEST QUAD TOUR

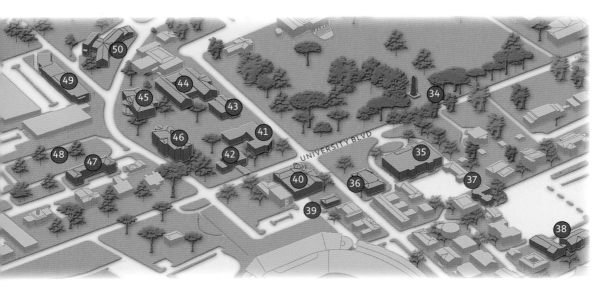

34   Denny Chimes

35   Rose Administration Building

36   Doster Hall

37   HES Design House

38   Barnwell Hall

39   Temple Tutwiler Hall

40   Reese Phifer Hall

41   Bibb Graves Hall

42   McLure Education Library

43   Carmichael Hall

44   Bidgood Hall

45   Alston Hall

46   Bruno Library and Bashinsky Computer Center

47   Friedman Hall

48   Presidential Dormitories (Demolished)

49   ten Hoor Hall

50   Rowand-Johnson Hall

34 DENNY CHIMES

During the antebellum period a bell in the cupola atop the Lyceum (now the site of Clark Hall [12]) was used to keep time. After the university changed to a military form of governance in 1860, a drum corps sounded the hours, and a bugler played reveille and taps and called cadets to meals in the Woods Hall dining room. From 1903, when the university abandoned the military form of governance, until the construction of Denny Chimes in 1929, students had to rely on their own alarm clocks and watches to get to classes on time.

The idea of building a bell tower or campanile was first suggested as a memorial to honor university students who had given their lives in World War I. Such structures, often containing chimes and large clocks, had become popular features on the nation's campuses. Because funds were not available at this time, the idea was dropped. (See "The Million Dollar Plan, 1925," p. 20.)

A decade later the tower was built, not as a war memorial but as a monument to President George Hutcheson Denny. Having heard rumors that the president contemplated leaving the university to return to his native Virginia, a group of Alabama students initiated a campaign to erect a campanile in his honor.

Miller, Martin, and Lewis designed the campanile, built of Alabama limestone and Virginia brick as a "token of respect for Dr. Denny's native state, Virginia."

The original carillon contained twenty-seven two-octave tubular bells that rang on the quarter hour. It featured an automatic player for musical programs and a manual keyboard for a carillonneur. The system functioned for sixteen years, until 1945, when it needed extensive repairs. It was then decided to replace it with an electric system that lasted until 1966. In that year a set of 305 bells was installed on the first floor. Loudspeakers in the belfry amplified the sounds. This system began to malfunction in the early 1980s.

A new carillon, installed in the belfry in the summer of 1986, cost about four times the price of the entire original monument. The twenty-five bells (bell-shaped this time), cast in Holland, range in weight from 60 to 1,411 pounds. Generous contributions from the alumni paid for this new system, optimistically expected to last for at least a century.

No one knows how it got started, but a legend is associated with the tower, and one generation of students passes it to the next. It asserts that bricks will fall from the monument on the head of any virgin who has the temerity to walk too near it.

Above: Denny Chimes

Right: The belfry contains a twenty-five-bell carillon.

Memorial Sidewalk

Since 1948 captains of the football team have placed their signatures, handprints, and cleated footprints in the slabs of concrete walkways surrounding Denny Chimes. In the first years of the century, the Alabama team was called the "Thin Red Line." Then, on October 5, 1919, a staff correspondent for the *Birmingham News,* reporting Alabama's 27 to 0 win over Birmingham-Southern College, stated that "the crimson tide of Alabama swept up and down a dust covered field for four touchdowns, while the Panthers of Birmingham-Southern College fought gamely and splendidly to stem the tide of defeat that was apparent from the kickoff." The "crimson tide" epithet stuck.

Memorial Trees

Many of the large oak trees overhanging University Boulevard along the side of the Quadrangle from Denny Chimes west to Campus Drive are memorial trees. Planted in 1921 by the Tuscaloosa post of the American Legion, they honor the men from Tuscaloosa County who gave their lives for their country in World War I. The trees once bore copper plaques (later replaced with marble) that identified each soldier. Over the years the plaques have disappeared because of vandalism and neglect. Many of the 1921 trees still stand and are registered with the US Forest Service in Washington, DC.

35 ROSE ADMINISTRATION BUILDING

As early as 1959 plans were begun to create an addition to the old 1925 Administration Building (now Carmichael Hall [43]). Subsequently, an entirely new structure was decided upon, one to be erected in another location. The site eventually chosen was, unfortunately, already occupied by historic Tutwiler Hall [22]. This handsome dormitory became the first major building to be demolished since the destruction of the school during the Civil War.

The controversial new administration building, completed in 1969 and named after President Frank Anthony Rose, was designed by McCowan and Knight, Architects (successors of Miller, Martin, and Lewis). The original design published in the June 4, 1967, *Tuscaloosa News* was entirely modern. However, public protests caused the board of trustees to advise the architects to alter the exterior of the building so that it would be more in harmony with the other structures. An editorial in the *News* on July 3, 1967, declared that "the Board of Trustees would be well advised to adopt a policy on architectural style in the campus core so that the present attractive and uniform appearance will not be marred by radical departures of modern design." It went on to state that "this decision will be applauded generally, for the main section of the campus has achieved a distinctive charm and grace which makes it one of the most attractive of any in the region." (The writer was intuitively responding to the *ensemble*—one of the fundamental principles

Rose Administration Building

of Beaux-Arts planning that promotes the idea that the whole is greater than the sum of its subordinate parts.)

After construction of the building the *Crimson-White* on February 23, 1970, stated that the "expensive $2-million structure has become a symbol of underlying discontent between the administration and faculty here." The earlier Greater University Development Campaign, which had pumped millions of federal dollars into new campus construction during the prosperous 1960s, had turned sour. Members of the faculty expressed the opinion that something was "radically wrong with the ranking of our priorities," adding that these funds should have been used for pressing academic needs rather than for new buildings, especially one to accommodate the administration.

36 DOSTER HALL

In 1929 Miller, Martin, and Lewis built Doster Hall to form one of the major components of the women's campus in the southwestern section of the campus. It was named after the dean of the College of Education, James J. Doster, and originally contained the departments of Fine Arts, Music, and Home Economics—disciplines considered suitable for study by women. It also housed classrooms, studios, and meeting rooms for various conferences and women's organizations over the state.

Courses in home economics were first offered at the university in 1914.

Doster Hall

By 1919, "home ec" had become a department, and in 1931, under the leadership of Dean Agnes Ellen Harris, the discipline was reorganized as the School of Home Economics. In 1987 it was renamed the College of Human Environmental Sciences. Three adjacent buildings were associated with this college: The HES Design House (slated for demolition) [37]; Harris Hall (located directly behind Doster—a living-learning community for HES students and other coeds with related interests); and Adams Hall. The latter was built as a west annex to now-demolished Tutwiler Hall [22] and contains HES Consumer Sciences, Interior Design, and Human Development and Family Studies.

37 HES DESIGN HOUSE

The HES Design House contained faculty offices and the Department of Clothing, Textiles, and Interior Design. The Neo-Georgian style structure had been built by Miller, Martin, and Lewis in 1939 as a Nursery School or Child Development Laboratory in which university students were given practical experience in caring for young children. The upstairs consisted of a "baby lab" for infants from three months to two years of age. The lower floor was designed to house two- to five-year-olds. The first nursery school on campus had been opened by Mrs. E. C. Springer, a graduate of Columbia University, in June 1931. A contemporary announcement stated that "tots range from 18 months to 5 years old and will be taught wholesome social

HES Design House

and mental habits." The Child Development Laboratory is now a part of the Child Development Research Center [87].

The HES Design House had been sheduled for demolition, and four large women's dormitories also designed by Miller, Martin, and Lewis—New Hall, Byrd, Adams-Parker, and Wilson halls, located east of this building—were previously razed to clear the area for a row of massive new sorority houses.

38 BARNWELL HALL

The first women's varsity basketball team had been formed in 1912 and won several games. In 1920 women were allowed to form another varsity basketball team named the Basketeers (changed a year later to the Crimsonettes), and in 1928 the university made plans to construct a gymnasium on the "Women's Campus." In 1931 the structure, built by the Birmingham architectural firm Warren, Knight, and Davis in a Classical Revival style, was named in honor of Charles H. Barnwell, dean of Arts and Sciences. That year, however, the university shifted emphasis in women's sports away from varsity athletics. Barnwell Hall and the playing field beside it soon became the sites of intramural basketball, swimming, baseball, archery, golf, horseback riding, horseshoes, soccer, tennis, and track. Apparently, tennis and golf teams did compete with other schools, but they were not considered to be varsity teams. Intramurals continued to be the mainstay of women's athletics until 1972 with the passage of Title IX, an amendment to the

Barnwell Hall

Education Act that made it against the law for schools and universities to discriminate against women in athletics. Barnwell Hall is now the home of University Printing Services.

39 TEMPLE TUTWILER HALL

Built in 1949 as the home of the Alumni Association, the structure was the gift of Temple Tutwiler, a member of the university's class of 1899, and a wealthy Birmingham businessman. University alumnus Paul Speake, also

Temple Tutwiler Hall

from Birmingham, was the architect. The ground floor included a large lobby and lounge as well as offices for the Alumni Association. Two apartments and a number of bedrooms were located on the second floor. The Alumni Association maintained its offices in this handsome Classical Revival building until 1987 when it moved to its present headquarters in Alumni Hall [95] adjacent to the Bryant Museum [96]. Temple Tutwiler Hall is currently the home of the Blackburn Institute and the Center for Ethics and Social Responsibility.

40 REESE PHIFER HALL

Formerly the Alabama Student Union Building, Reese Phifer Hall was dedicated in 1930 as a "memorial to all former University of Alabama students who have borne arms in defense of their state or their country." It featured the usual Miller, Martin, and Lewis hallmarks, including the raised basement and the classical Tuscan Doric portico. Like Farrah Hall [31] to the east and the contemporaneous Bibb Graves Hall [41] to the north, its major entrance was on the corner of the structure. And, like Farrah Hall, it was approached by a monumental flight of Alabama limestone stairs. Coeds rarely used this entrance because of a persistent legend that only women of dubious virtue dared to climb these steps. Gusty winds may have been at the root of this tradition. When dress codes for women were abandoned in the early 1970s, the taboo was forgotten. Many alumnae still remember the strict regulations governing female attire. Slacks or shorts were permissible only

Reese Phifer Hall

for specified occasions. In the 1960s women art students, for example, were allowed to wear pants to art class, but to get to Woods Hall or Garland Hall from their dormitories or sorority houses—no matter what the weather—they were forced to wear raincoats. Some students used this regulation to their advantage. One alumna in the late 1950s had difficulty meeting her early morning English composition class because of chronic oversleeping. She solved the problem with a raincoat. If she skipped breakfast and slept late, it was still possible to jump out of bed, roll up her pajama legs, pull on her raincoat, and make her nine o'clock class in Morgan Hall [19] (the student received her BA degree twenty-two years later).

The Union Building was renovated in 1980 and is now the home of the College of Communications and Information Sciences. In 1991 it was renamed Reese Phifer Hall to honor a University of Alabama alumnus, Tuscaloosa businessman, and philanthropist.

41 BIBB GRAVES HALL

Bibb Graves Hall, built to house the College of Education, was dedicated in 1929 and named in honor of Governor Bibb Graves. A Warren, Knight, and Davis design, its main entrance is on the corner facing the intersection of University Boulevard and Colonial Drive. One enters at ground level through a massive engaged portico of Ionic columns. Above the entablature and cornice is a stone attic, in the manner of a Roman triumphal arch, bearing an inscription from the famous 1787 Northwest Ordinance: "Re-

Bibb Graves Hall

ligion, morality, and knowledge being necessary to good government and the happiness of mankind, schools and the means of education shall forever be encouraged." This ordinance established the precedent that new states entering the Union would enter on an equal footing with the original states, and that revenue generated from the sale of a portion of each township in a state would go to fund public education—the first example of federal aid to education in US history. These words were also a part of Alabama's first constitution.

The building underwent major renovation in 2006 and is still in use by the College of Education.

McLure Library

42 MCLURE EDUCATION LIBRARY

McLure Education Library, built in 1925 by Miller, Martin, and Lewis, was originally the university Post Office and Supply Store. In the late nineteenth century the former had been operated out of one of the lower floor rooms in the Gorgas House [8] by postmistress Amelia Gayle Gorgas, and later it was moved to the first floor of Woods Hall [11]. The new post office in McLure and the soda fountain in the university Supply Store were popular meeting places for students in the 1920s and 1930s. The basement of the structure housed a large student cafeteria that took over the functions of the old dining room in Woods Hall.

In 1954 the old building was remodeled to house the College of Education Library, which still occupies it, and in 1975 it was named after John Rankin McLure, dean of that college from 1942 to 1959.

43 CARMICHAEL HALL

The first Amelia Gayle Gorgas Library (now Carmichael Hall) was designed and built by Miller, Martin, and Lewis in 1925. It was intended to serve as a temporary library until funds to erect a larger structure could be secured. It was then to be converted into an administration building. Initially, only the lower floor was used for administration. The building is similar in scale and design to Nott Hall [27] directly across the Quadrangle.

The upper two floors housed the library until the completion of the present Amelia Gayle Gorgas Library [24]. It had a capacity of about sixty thousand books in stacks kept closed to students. The general reading room, containing current periodicals, occupied the whole front section of the third floor.

Carmichael Hall

After the library was moved to its new quarters in 1940, the building served as the administrative headquarters for the university until the construction of Rose Administration Building [35] in 1969. In 1971 the old building was renamed Carmichael Hall in honor of President Oliver Cromwell Carmichael. Occupied since 1995 by the School of Education, it houses educational programs as well as the office of the dean of the college.

44 BIDGOOD HALL

Bidgood Hall, built in 1928, is the oldest of four buildings occupied by the Culverhouse College of Commerce and Business Administration. It is named after Lee Bidgood who served as the first dean of the college. After undergoing a major renovation in 1994 the structure now houses many of the college's classrooms and student services. The Alabama Business Hall of Fame is located on the first floor just inside the main entrance and features pictures and memorabilia.

Although Miller, Martin, and Lewis designed it, the building differs in some respects from their usual formula. The projecting Classical Revival portico of Roman Ionic columns is there, but it is not raised on a stone podium or base. Instead, the portico begins at ground level and runs through the full three-story height of the building. The double flight of exterior stairs is still present, but in this example of the firm's classical formula it is under

the portico and leads to a deeply inset landing flanked by Adamesque oval   Bidgood Hall
windows. The red brick of the building is emphasized on the first floor by a
continuous blind arcade pierced by large rectangular windows.

45 ALSTON HALL

Located directly behind Bidgood Hall, Alston Hall, a large new addition to
the College of Commerce and Business Administration, was constructed in
1989. It was made possible by a generous bequest from the estate of Robert
Nabors Alston, a Tuscaloosa financier and businessman, and named in
honor of his mother, Mary Hewell Alston.

Alston Hall contains offices of the faculty and administrators of the
college as well as large student classrooms.

The building was designed by David Volkert and Associates of Mobile in
a Postmodern style. Typical of some variations of this late twentieth-century
architectural style, the building features "classical," but highly stylized references—a raised basement, a semicircular monumental portico whose stripped
entablature lacks moldings and cornice, Tuscan Doric columns (without entasis or abaci above their capitals), and a gigantic overscale fanlight in the
pediment. Despite its "modernity" and somewhat busy facade, Alston Hall
is a good neighbor and, thanks to careful manipulation of scale and proportions, fits in with the older, more traditional buildings that surround it.

Alston Hall

Bruno Library and
Bashinsky Computer
Center

46 BRUNO LIBRARY AND BASHINSKY COMPUTER CENTER

The Culverhouse College of Business Administration's Library and Computer Center opened in 1994. It was named in honor of two benefactors to the university: Angelo Bruno and Sloan Y. Bashinsky Sr., both prominent Alabama businessmen. Janus-like, the structure has two main entrances. Located in what was once considered an area unsuitable for construction—a depression behind the buildings on the western side of the Quad—campus planners sited and configured the three-story building in such a way that it forms a minor cross axis to the original plan of the central campus. The eastern facade of the structure, designed by the Montgomery firm of PH&J Architects Inc., features an arcaded entrance into the Bashinsky Computer Center under a pedimented portico of Ionic columns. The open space

Friedman Hall

in front, partially enclosed by the older buildings, creates a pleasant small quadrangle. Because the building backs into a slope, the western elevation is only two stories high. One enters the second story Bruno Library through a street-level monumental Ionic portico.

The interior features a spiral staircase connecting all three floors and is capped by an internal dome (not visible from the exterior) surmounted by a copper cupola or lantern that illuminates the handsome interior.

From an architectural standpoint this building is one of the most successful "in fills" in the central campus. Yet while its general design, scale, and arrangement are sensitive to its surroundings, the details lack the finesse and subtlety found on the older structures on the main Quad built by architects trained in the Beaux-Arts traditions of the earlier part of the twentieth century.

47 Friedman Hall

Friedman Hall was built in 1951 as a dormitory for athletes and named to honor Hugo Friedman, a local businessman, benefactor of the university, and avid football fan. Athletes later moved to a new home officially dedicated as Paul W. Bryant Hall in 1965. Friedman Hall was later renovated as a residential community for the exclusive use of men and women enrolled in the nearby Culverhouse College of Business Administration.

48 Presidential Dormitories (Demolished)

In 1939 PWA funds allowed the construction of much-needed men's dormitories. Six designed by Miller, Martin, and Lewis in a restrained, Neo-Georgian style were located behind the academic buildings located on the west side of the main Quadrangle. Wyman, Lupton, Lewis, Clayton, Jones, and Powers halls were named after former university presidents. For seventy

The Presidential Dormitories were demolished in 2010.

years these sturdy, well-proportioned buildings served as homes away from home for thousands of students before their demolition in 2010.

49 TEN HOOR HALL

The completion of the social sciences building in 1963 was hailed as the beginning of a new era for the College of Arts and Sciences by Professor Marten ten Hoor, dean emeritus of the college, after whom the building was eventually named.

Edwin McCowan of the firm Miller, Martin, Lewis, and Edwin T. McCowan, was faced with a difficult problem because the site chosen was just below the brow of one of the deep ravines cutting through this section of campus. The location dictated that the lower floor of this four-story building be built into the side of the hill. In an attempt to relate this essentially functional, modern building to its neighbors, the architect applied Neo-Georgian elements to the center of the building, creating the look of a rather bloated Palladian villa with flat-topped, elongated north and south wings. Despite its ungainly appearance—which suggests the effect of a building slowly sliding down the hill—ten Hoor Hall provided much-needed classrooms, seminar rooms, and offices for various departments within the College of Arts and Sciences, including American studies, anthropology, history, philosophy, and political science.

50 ROWAND-JOHNSON HALL

Formerly known as the Music and Speech Building, Rowand-Johnson Hall was constructed in 1956 by Paul Speake, an architect of Van Keuren, Davis, and Company of Birmingham. Because all the proposed locations on the old Million Dollar Plan had been used, it was built on the edge of a steep hill

ten Hoor Hall

Rowand-Johnson Hall

behind Comer [18] and Morgan [19] halls, a difficult site. Speake attempted to blend it in by utilizing classical details, including a massive Greek Doric portico in the center, flanked by canted wings that follow the contours of the hill. Interestingly, the building is the only purely Greek Revival structure on campus. Other "classical" campus structures with their raised basements, arches, arcades, and sweeping stairs reflect Roman and even Renaissance interpretations of the classical orders. The central entrance leads into the lobby of the 338-seat Marian Gallaway Theatre, named in honor of the director of Theatre from 1948 to 1973. The long east and west wings of the structure were originally designed to house classrooms, practice rooms, studios, and offices for the Music and Speech departments. The building is now home to the Department of Communicative Disorders and the Department of Theatre and Dance. In 1989 it was renamed in honor of Dr. T. Earle Johnson, a former chairman of the Department of Speech, and Dr. Wilbur Rowand, a former chairman of the Department of Music.

TOUR 6

SCIENCE AND ENGINEERING CORRIDOR TOUR

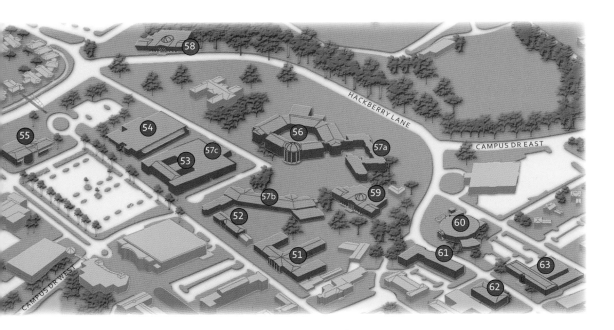

51	Hardaway Hall
52	Houser Hall
53	Mineral Industries Building (Hugh Moss Comer Hall)
54	Bevill Building
55	AIME Building
56	Shelby Hall
57a	Science and Engineering Building
57b	South Engineering Research Center
57c	North Engineering Research Center
58	National Water Center Research Building
59	Rodgers Library for Science and Engineering
60	Biology Building
61	Walter Bryan Jones Hall
62	Mary Harmon Bryant Hall
63	Gordon Palmer Hall

51 HARDAWAY HALL

The College of Engineering had completely outgrown its quarters in Comer Hall [18] by 1930, but it was not possible to build a new building until 1936, when funds became available from the Public Works Administration. Following the Million Dollar Plan (see fig. 15), the new structure was erected by Miller, Martin, and Lewis due east of Comer Hall. According to that plan, Woods Hall [11], standing between the two, was to be removed, but in the end it was saved.

The building was named after Colonel Robert A. Hardaway, who became the university's first full-time engineering professor in 1882. Although the subject had been taught at the school for nearly half a century, earlier en-

Hardaway Hall

gineering professors taught in other disciplines as well. Hardaway Hall is home to the Department of Mechanical Engineering and the Department of Aerospace Engineering and Mechanics.

52 HOUSER HALL

Hauser Hall, the third large engineering building to be built on the campus, was completed by Miller, Martin, and Lewis in 1950 and named after Shaler C. Houser, university treasurer, bursar, and professor of Civil Engineering from 1912 to 1948. To relate this structure to the earlier Hardaway Hall the architectural firm constructed the facade with a similar centered, pedimented monumental Tuscan Doric portico.

Hauser Hall is home to the Department of Computer Science and the Department of Electrical and Computer Engineering.

Houser Hall

53 Mineral Industries Building (Hugh Moss Comer Hall)

The Mineral Industries Building, completed in 1962, was the first new engineering building to be built after the adoption of the 1961 General Development Plan (see "The General Development Plan," p. 27). Designed by the firm Miller, Martin, Lewis & Edwin T. McCowan, it was named after the late Hugh Moss Comer, a Birmingham industrialist who had served as the Greater University Development Campaign's first chairman. The university's engineering building, Comer Hall [18], had been named after Hugh Moss Comer's father, Governor Braxton Bragg Comer. Two Comer Halls on campus led to considerable confusion and frustration on the part of countless students attempting to decipher their class schedules, and Hugh

Mineral Industries
Building

Moss Comer Hall has been for years commonly called the Mineral Industries Building.

Dr. Wernher von Braun from the Marshall Space Flight Center in Huntsville dedicated Hugh Moss Comer Hall during a two-day symposium on engineering education. Von Braun stated that the building was "an appropriate launch site for a projection into the future." He noted that one of the most pressing needs plaguing the space program for years was "more trained engineers." He observed that in Russia 39 percent of engineers were women, and he recommended that more women enter American programs. A few women had enrolled in the College of Engineering at the university as early as the 1920s, but their numbers did not increase significantly until the 1970s.

The Mineral Industries Building houses the Engineering Student Services office, Capstone Engineering Society, and the office of the dean of the College of Engineering.

54 BEVILL BUILDING

Visible to the north of the Mineral Industries Building is the first major energy research center to be built in the southeast, and the university's first facility dedicated solely to research. It was a cost-sharing venture between the university and the US Department of Energy. The Tom Bevill Energy, Mineral, and Material Science Research Building was completed in 1990 and named in honor of Congressman Tom Bevill of Alabama's Fourth Dis-

Bevill Building

trict, who played a key role in obtaining federal funds to build it, as well as the nearby AIME [55] Building. The Benham Group, Inc., of Oklahoma City and Evan M. Terry Associates of Birmingham were the architects of this Modernist building. In comparison with other campus structures it is notable for the total absence of columns or any other classical references.

55 AIME BUILDING

The Alabama Institute for Manufacturing Excellence (AIME) was created in 1995, bringing together faculty from numerous academic areas, including the colleges of Engineering, Arts and Sciences, and Business. It is a research center directly tied to improving the state's manufacturing processes and to preparing university students for manufacturing-related careers.

The building, designed by KPS Group, Inc., of Birmingham and built in 1999, incorporates areas used for distance education/teleconferencing, which allow manufacturing companies across the state to meet the needs of their workers. It also contains offices, labs, conference rooms, and a "high bay" area with a 35-foot ceiling allowing the setup of industrial-size equipment enabling university professors to "monitor and offer solutions to specific manufacturing problems a company is facing."

The original Modernist design of the AIME Building reflected the intended, basically industrial use of the structure. When presented with the design, the board of trustees, in keeping with a national trend on some college campuses toward more traditionally styled buildings and also the waning influence of Modernism, requested modifications to make it "fit in" with the rest of the campus. In some respects the redesign was quite clever, though its wittiness is lost on most viewers. The general massing, red brick

AIME Building

and white trim, and emphatic belt courses relate it to the nearby purely Modernist Bevill Building to the east. However, to relate it to the older, traditional, columned Classical Revival buildings the architects came up with a Postmodern solution. Rather than using the traditional orders, they created columns from iron pipes—plates, nuts, and bolts taking the place of the various parts of the classical column. Other "classical" allusions in modern materials also remind the viewer of the campus's older buildings.

56 SHELBY HALL

Many research universities across the country built large science and engineering complexes during the last quarter of the twentieth century, but lacking resources, Alabama lagged behind, and it was only in the first decade of the twenty-first century that federal funds made costly new research buildings possible.

Shelby Hall, the anchor facility of the university's science and engineering buildings, was dedicated on May 14, 2004. While it provided much needed new research facilities for the Department of Chemistry formerly located in Lloyd Hall [26], Shelby Hall also houses a variety of interdisciplinary science programs. Designed as a pentagon, the two wings on either side of the 80-foot tall entry rotunda contain teaching facilities while the northern three wings are dedicated to research.

The idea of constructing a new chemistry building that crossed academic boundaries was developed by President Andrew Sorensen in the late 1990s. Realizing that the large amount of money necessary to create such a structure would not be forthcoming from the state government, he turned to Congress and solicited the aid of Senator Richard Shelby, an Alabama alumnus who was able to arrange a substantial federal contribution to the project. Designed by North America's largest architectural firm, HOK Inc., the design of the building underwent many costly changes over the next several years. The earliest plans depicted a fairly conventional Modernist building, but later versions reflected a national trend toward Neo-Traditional architecture. (Neo-Traditional architecture, or Postmodern "Canonic Classicism" as it is also known, acknowledges the principles and aesthetics of past architectural forms and forthrightly employs them in new buildings. This differs from the "Ironic Classical" variant of Postmodernism [employed on the AIME Building] in which architects—even though they often quote traditional forms—seem compelled to play about with them in the hope of producing something whimsical and "new.")

From Top:

An aerial rendering of Shelby Hall and the Science and Engineering Complex.

A view of Shelby Hall (left), and the Science and Engineering Building (center and right).

Shelby Hall

According to sources quoted in a November 23, 2003, article in the *Mobile Register,* Shelby and his wife Annette, in honor of whom the university named the new structure, are recorded as having asked that the university design "something like" the Ronald W. Reagan Building and International Trade Center in Washington, DC. Other Washington "references," though probably unintentional, are the Pentagon and the Jefferson Memorial.

At first glance Shelby Hall appears to be an orthodox and even academic rendering of classical forms, but on closer inspection, one realizes that the colossal Tuscan Doric columns supporting the base of the domed rotunda and those on the projecting porticos lack abaci (an abacus is the square block placed atop the capital of a Doric column to support the architrave of the entablature above). This Postmodernist "tinkering" with a classical order is also evident on Alston Hall [45] and the Child Development Research Center [87]. Even more curious is the fact that the architects, who broke one of the most fundamental rules of columnar architecture, also recessed these unusual columns under the architrave rather than aligning them on the same vertical plane with the base of the building and with the entablature above them. These presumably intentional deviations from classical conventions, especially evident in the porticos on the wings, give parts of the otherwise traditionally designed building an awkward and clumsy effect. It is interesting to note that the architects of the contiguous Science and Engineering Complex [57] built some years later, did not repeat these anomalies, but, instead, employed more harmonious classical proportions consistent with the rest of the large buildings.

57 SCIENCE AND ENGINEERING COMPLEX

The Science and Engineering Building [57a], designed by Davis Architects of Birmingham, located to the south of and connected to Shelby Hall, opened in 2009. Following current educational trends it is an interdisciplinary building housing all freshman chemistry labs, teaching and research labs, faculty and student offices from the chemical and biological engineering and computer science departments, science teaching labs for the College of Education, and space for the Science in Motion biology program.

The South Engineering Research Center [57b], also designed by Davis Architects, was completed in January 2012. It is dedicated solely to the College of Engineering and contains laboratories dedicated to study applications in fuels and combustion research. In addition the building contains

From Top:

South Engineering
Research Center

Rendering of the
North Engineering
Research Center

Science and Engineer-
ing Building

offices for five of the college's departments as well as classrooms, labs, conference rooms, and offices for faculty and graduate students.

The North Engineering Research Center [57c], located behind the
Mineral Industries Building (Hugh Moss Comer Hall [53]), designed by
Williams Blackstock Architects from Birmingham, was completed in 2013.
It houses additional research laboratories, faculty and graduate student of-
fices, conference rooms, and collaborative spaces.

Rendering of the
National Water Center
Research Building

58 NATIONAL WATER CENTER RESEARCH BUILDING

In 2011 the university leased a portion of the former Bryce Hospital Property
to the US Department of Commerce's National Oceanic and Atmospheric
Administration (NOAA) to construct a building to house a national hydro-
logic operations center, support services, and the administrative functions of
NOAA's National Weather Service. The structure, one of a number of such
buildings located across the country, monitors water resources and provides
forecast information. Located on campus it also provides faculty and students the opportunity to collaborate with the twenty-four federal agencies
that perform water-related research.

The center, featuring a sweeping arcade of Tuscan Doric columns and a
large dome, was designed by Kansas City, Missouri, architects Gould Evans,
Associates, LC.

59 RODGERS LIBRARY FOR SCIENCE AND ENGINEERING

Design of the science and engineering library, whose construction began
in 1989, presented a challenge due to the rapid changes taking place in the
creation, distribution, storage, and retrieval of information. To meet these
challenges, the architects, Evan Terry Associates PC of Birmingham, were
charged with creating a building with "maximum flexibility in design .
. . so that the facility may be adapted to changes in technology and in the
provision of library services." The library was named after Eric and Sarah
Rodgers. Dr. Rodgers had served as professor and head of the Department
of Physics and later as dean of the Graduate School. Mrs. Rodgers was an
assistant professor of business administration.

Although contemporary descriptions of the new building referred to it as "traditionally styled" with a dome "reminiscent of the dome on the Rotunda [1]," the design of the Rodgers Library is an example of the "Ironic Classical" variant of Postmodernism. Rather than build a traditional temple-like building, the architects—employing a five-part Palladian villa footprint—created a witty entrance portico featuring a flat, almost billboard-like, stylized, and semiabstract semiotic "signal" that suggests (but clearly is not) a classical pediment replete with acroteria, placed above Tuscan Doric columns. The Rodgers Library with its playful but sophisticated manipulation and exaggeration of classical forms engages in a somewhat cheeky Postmodernist conversation with its more traditional and conservative neighbors.

The same cannot be said, however, about the nearby Campus Drive parking deck and intermodal facility built in 2004 by the same architectural

Left: Rodgers Library for Science and Engineering

Below: Campus Drive Parking Deck

Biology Building

firm. In a misguided attempt to make it look less like a utilitarian structure the designers dressed it up with "classical" forms—awkwardly and artlessly appliquéd to what could have been a relatively inconspicuous and inoffensive functional building. Rather than blending in with the surrounding structures, the cacophony of misunderstood classical details on the building calls attention to itself.

60 BIOLOGY BUILDING

In November 1968 President Rose announced that a new biology building would be constructed. The original design, as reflected in the 1961 General Development Plan, called for a conventional, rectangular structure, but a circular configuration was eventually deemed more practical. The unusual building, as finally designed by the Birmingham architectural firm of Warren, Knight, and Davis, has a central core arrangement for corridors and utilities, with classrooms and laboratories arranged around the perimeter.

Columns (or more accurately piers), apparently added to the original design, were a misguided attempt to relate it to the other campus buildings. The two badly scaled and poorly proportioned porticos (the shafts of the piers are not tapered, nor do they exhibit entasis) created a great deal of controversy on January 11, 1971, when the *Crimson-White* ran a photograph of the nearly completed structure with the caption: "For a reported $60,000,

the University has seen fit to build a facade on the biology building. . . . The columns are without purpose being constructed only to 'conform' to other buildings dotting the area landscape." In a later issue the paper printed a full-page tongue-in-cheek photographic collage of campus "columns" and challenged its readers to identify the buildings to which they belonged.

Walter Bryan Jones Hall

Despite its ungainly exterior, however, the interior of the Biology Building proved to be quite functional and efficient and still provides space for some of that department's programs.

61 WALTER BRYAN JONES HALL

"This is a great day for all Alabama and it will be a landmark in the development of Alabama resources," declared Governor John M. Patterson on May 4, 1962, as he formally dedicated Walter Bryan Jones Hall, the Oil and Gas Board Building located on the university campus. It was designed by architect Martin J. Lide and named after Professor Jones, who had served as state geologist from 1927 to 1961 and oil and gas supervisor from 1945 to 1961. Although part of the university community, the building is owned by the state. The Oil and Gas Board is a regulatory agency with the statutory charge of preventing waste and promoting the conservation of oil and gas while ensuring the protection of the environment and the rights of landowners.

Mary Harmon Bryant
Hall

62 MARY HARMON BRYANT HALL

Originally known as the Scientific Collections Facility when it was constructed in 1994, the structure was designed by the Birmingham architectural firm of Garikes Wilson Atkinson, Inc., to serve as a central depository
for the university's scientific and historic collections. In 2001 it was named
Mary Harmon Bryant Hall to honor Mary Harmon Black Bryant, an
alumna of the university and wife of former head football coach, Paul W.
"Bear" Bryant.

The first floor of the building contains rock samples and drilling cores belonging to the Alabama State Oil and Gas Board/Geological Survey whose
headquarters are located in the building next door, Walter Bryan Jones Hall
[61].

The second floor houses the W. S. Hoole Special Collections Library
formerly located in the Gorgas Library [24]. It contains rare books and
materials relating to Alabama and the Deep South, Confederate imprints,
pamphlets, maps, and an extensive collection of manuscripts. Of particular
interest are archives of the university and various artifacts pertaining to the
history of the school.

The third floor contains the Alabama Museum of Natural History's rich
paleontology, mineralogy, entomology, ornithology, mammalogy, ethnology,
osteology, history, and photographic collections.

The Department of Biological Sciences utilizes the fourth floor to house a
herbarium and ichthyology, herpetology, and mollusk collections.

The building is essentially an enormous box with awkwardly proportioned classical details. The focal point of its facade, however, is a handsome Tiffany memorial window. (For a history of this window see "Memorial Window," p. 41.)

Gordon Palmer Hall

63 GORDON PALMER HALL

The mathematics-psychology building, a 1967 construction named for a university trustee who served from 1940 to 1956, was made possible by a matching-fund grant from the Department of Health, Education, and Welfare. Home to the departments of Mathematics and Psychology, and the Office of Information Technology, the building was designed by Birmingham architect Wilmot C. Douglas in an abbreviated Neo-Georgian style with a slightly projecting central block dominated by a recessed portico. The portico is supported by disproportionately elongated stone piers and capped by a semicircular pediment similar to the one at the entrance of nearby Gallalee Hall [28]. The central block is flanked by north and south wings that terminate in windowless end pavilions.

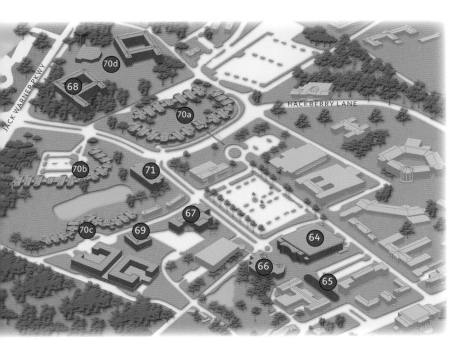

64   Ferguson Center

65   Crimson Promenade

66   Student Services Center

67   Paty Hall

68   Rose Towers (Demolished)

69   Blount Living-Learning Center

70a   Riverside Residential Community

70b   Lakeside Residential Community

70c   Ridgecrest Residential Community

70d   Presidential Village Residential Community

71   Lakeside Dining Hall, Palmer Lake

72   Tutwiler Hall

64 FERGUSON CENTER

Although it was not actually completed until 1973, plans for the construction of a new student center to replace the Student Union (now Reese Phifer Hall [40]) were begun almost a decade earlier. A portion of student activity fees had long been set aside for that purpose. In 1966, when it was discovered that Woods Hall [11] was on the list of proposed sites for the new building, concerned students and alumni launched a "Save Woods Hall" campaign. The location eventually chosen for the new center was immediately north of Woods Hall on the site of Dressler Hall, a wooden intramural sports facility destroyed by arsonists on May 7, 1970.

The construction of Ferguson Center, named in honor of Hill Ferguson, one of the originators of the Greater University Plan over half a century earlier and a longtime member of the board of trustees, shifted the center of campus activities from University Boulevard to the northern part of campus. Designed by Pearson, Tittle, Narrows, and Associates of Montgomery, the structure was advertised at its opening as the "Living Room of the South." Rather than a "historic" style, the architects chose to employ a completely modern idiom. Typical of many buildings constructed in the 1970s, the Ferguson Center was almost totally nonreferential and ignored its older neighbors designed in the Gothic Revival, Victorian, and Classical Revival styles. As originally constructed it consisted of enormous cantilevered slabs of reinforced concrete held up by steel reinforced concrete pillars. Curtain walls of unadorned brick and narrow glass windows enclosed the structure. The interior was divided into a basement with two floors above, but parts of the first story were two-story in height, including a cavernous dining area. (Over the years various attempts were made to make this space more inviting and less noisy. Cloth banners to absorb sound were suspended from the ceiling, upholstered furniture was also introduced for the same purpose and the red brick and raw concrete were painted, and cast iron light fixtures removed.) Although its interior had been modified in piecemeal fashion over the years to rectify various shortcomings, it was the major 1998–2000 Postmodernist remodeling (based on the revised 1993 Campus Master Plan) that, if it did not solve, at least toned down the building's "attitude" problem toward the surrounding older structures. The creation of truncated flat-topped towers on the west side broke up the monotony of the enormous flat roof and the oval arcade and terraces related it to the new Student Services Center [66] on the other side of the plaza. The remodeling also provided space on the main floor for additional dining areas for 450 people and a coffee bar. A somewhat later addition to the north side enclosed a

Right: Original south facade of Ferguson Center

Below: Rendering of the remodeled south facade of the Ferguson Center

seldom-used windswept porch with a wall of glass and provided even more dining space for the rapidly growing student population. The most recent 2013 addition to the south side by TurnerBatson Architects now completely encases the original building.

The oval plaza between Ferguson Center and the Student Services Center also softened the rigidity and angularity of the building and opened up what had been the basement home of the post office and Supe Store to the out of doors. The plaza features a fountain in the center that can be programmed to spurt elaborately choreographed water jets in interesting patterns. Like many modern fountains it does not have a basin and the water almost magically disappears into grills set into the concrete plaza. Several conventional fountains with basins had been erected on campus over the years, but all have been removed. The last was located in front of Rose Administration Building [35]. The major problem was that Alabama fans dumped Tide detergent in them and the suds eventually destroyed the pump mechanisms. The Ferguson fountain has so far proved to be Tide proof.

Crimson Promenade

65 CRIMSON PROMENADE

In 1999 a four-lane road, McCorvey Drive—a misguided "improvement" built in the early 1970s that encouraged traffic congestion in the central campus area—was closed to create a pedestrian mall. It was one of several changes brought about by the Campus Master Plan that was updated that year and that reemphasized the desirability for a pedestrian central campus. The Crimson Promenade is paved with hundreds of bricks inscribed with the names of and messages from Alabama alumni and friends. Although only a step above graffiti, the use of inscribed bricks for such projects is a popular phenomenon across the country and sales of the pavers provided funds to pay for the walkway's construction and several student leadership projects.

The north end of the promenade terminates with a vine-covered pergola while the south contains a memorial gate erected to commemorate the university's 175th anniversary. Its form echoes that of a much less durable wooden picket affair (see fig. 6) that once marked the entrance to the south end of the university grounds facing the Huntsville Road now known as University Boulevard.

66 STUDENT SERVICES CENTER

In the late 1990s the architects KPS Group, Inc., of Birmingham were faced with the challenge of creating a building that would somehow act as a transition between the stark, uncompromising rectilinear Modernism of the Ferguson Center and the more complex and ornamental detailing of the older surrounding buildings. The result, an example of Postmodernist contextualization, is surprisingly successful. The polychromy and texture refer to the

Student Services
Center

Victorian buildings, and the arcades and stone roundels are reminiscent of nearby Comer Hall [18]. Even the simple modernist iron railings have inset semiotic "baluster" patterns referencing those on older academic campus buildings.

67 PATY HALL

Before the construction of the enormous residence communities in this area during the first years of the twenty-first century, the north campus was dominated by Paty Hall and Rose Towers [68]. The largest men's dormitory on campus, Paty Hall, built by Birmingham architect Wilmot C. Douglas and Tuscaloosa architect Carl M. Moseley Jr., was dedicated at homecoming 1962 and named after Dr. Raymond Ross Paty, who had served as university president immediately following World War II. The timing of Paty's construction was unfortunate. Despite the influx of baby boomers in the 1960s it proved difficult to keep the dormitory fully occupied. Over the years more and more students brought cars to campus, and it became the fashion for men, if at all possible, to live off campus, even if one's "apartment" consisted of nothing more than a former garage in someone's backyard. The situation became so dire that in 1972 the university leased Paty Hall to the Alabama Department of Mental Health for use as a transitional facility for patients leaving Partlow State School who were to be returned to community settings. The program was not successful, however, and Paty was once again turned back into a dormitory. By the 1980s it had undergone several renovations that made it more attractive to students. These included reducing

Paty Hall

Rose Towers was
demolished in 2012.

the number of residents per floor and providing more amenities. In 1984
University Housing designated that the top two floors would be reserved
"for engineering students and students in other particularly demanding disciplines. . . . The student who wants a 24-hour study environment will have
that available." This was an early experiment with discipline-based residence
halls, which have become popular in the twenty-first century.

68 ROSE TOWERS (DEMOLISHED)

Like Paty Hall, Rose Towers had a checkered past. Built by the Birmingham
firm of McCowan and Knight Architects (successor to Miller, Martin,
Lewis & McCowan) and the Knoxville firm of Good & Goodstein, Inc.,
and named after Tommye Stuart Rose, wife of university president Frank

A. Rose, this Modernist thirteen-story structure containing three hundred apartments opened in 1969 as housing for married students. Since the end of World War II these students and their families had had to make do with increasingly dilapidated PWA and World War II "temporary" housing stock located on campus at Ridgecrest, at the old Northington General Army Hospital (now the site of University Mall), and at Bakersfield off Tenth Street (now Bryant Drive) where some families in the 1950s were housed in trailers.

Rose Towers was quite popular initially, but within a few years it fell out of favor due to extensive apartment building by Tuscaloosa developers. To meet bond payments on the structure the university was forced to open two wings to undergraduates, reserving only one wing for married students and graduates. The building was demolished in 2012, to be replaced by an expansion of the Presidential Village (Phase II) Residential Community.

69 BLOUNT LIVING-LEARNING CENTER

By the beginning of the twenty-first century the university followed a national trend by referring to dormitories as "Residence Halls," "Residential Communities," or, as here, a "Living-Learning Center." A number of older dormitories around campus had been refurbished to accommodate this new type of domicile (Friedman Hall [47] is an example), but the four-story Blount Living-Learning Center, which opened in 2000, was the first such structure built on campus.

The unusual-looking building was designed by the Atlanta architectural firm of Niles Bolton Associates. In an attempt to relate it to the Blount program's classroom buildings, Tuomey [15] and Oliver-Barnard [16] halls, on the Main Quad, the architects applied rather awkward, stylized "Victorian" details to an otherwise conventional modern residential structure.

Blount Living-Learning Center

70 RESIDENTIAL COMMUNITIES

President Robert Witt's plan to increase enrollment at the university required construction of new residence halls to house the anticipated influx of students. The first of a series of such structures was built in 2005 north of the AIME Building [55]. Named Riverside [70a] this group of buildings, like the later Lakeside [70b] and Ridgecrest [70c] residence halls, is an enormous housing project. Architects were HADP Architecture, Inc., of Atlanta, and WSV, Architects of Tuscaloosa. Modern multistory campus residential complexes do not lend themselves easily to historical styles. Red brick veneer and quoins give these massive boxlike structures a vaguely Neo-Georgian effect. However, their fifth stories, clad in white stucco, feature awkward and badly scaled "classical" details that are distracting.

Brobdingnagian in its proportions, Ridgecrest South [70c] opened in 2009 and was on completion the second largest structure on campus. Only Bryant-Denny Stadium was larger. Beneath this behemoth is a 950-space, three-story parking garage. The height of this eight-story building complex is somewhat disguised by the fact that it is built into the side of a ravine. Here again, portions of the buildings including the topmost stories are clad in light stucco and, while the classical details are somewhat better articulated, pilaster-clad pedimented projections cantilevered into space five

Riverside Residential
Community

Fom Top:

Lakeside Residential
Community

Ridgecrest Residential
Community

Rendering of the
Presidential Village
Residential Commu-
nity

stories above viewers' heads defy all sense of logic and architectural design. Despite their aesthetic shortcomings, these residential communities are well appointed and even luxurious in their interiors.

In 2010 the board of trustees approved the construction of the Presidential Village Residential Community [70d], an even larger student housing complex located east of the now-demolished Rose Towers [68]. The following year the trustees approved plans to demolish Rose Towers and build on its site an expansion of the Presidential Village Residential Community, a new dining facility, and a recreation center. After the violent April 27, 2011, tornado, the architects incorporated a large three-thousand-person FEMA-compliant storm shelter in the plans.

Residents of these twenty-first-century structures will appreciate their amenities even more after reading the following description published in the January 1940 *Alumni News* of the earlier, Spartan, frame dormitories that were once located on the Ridgecrest site, although parents may be more impressed by the costs of seventy-three years ago:

> Eleven neat and comfortable dormitories have already been constructed at Ridge Crest in a WPA project of 20 buildings. Each will accommodate 20 boys, and rent is only $4.50 per month. Each dormitory has a sleeping porch, 10 study rooms which the boys share in pairs, and a recitation-reading room. The study rooms are each equipped with two maple topped dressers, two desks and two closets. Each building has its own large bath room with showers, wash basins and mirrors. Many rooms have small desk radios but to eliminate too much "static" a number of houses have established quiet hours, usually from 2 to 5 in the afternoon and 8 to 11 at night. . . . A dining hall is also nearly completed. . . . It is estimated that good board will be available for as little as $13.50 a month which, when Ridge Crest is completed, will allow 400 students to receive room and board for $18 monthly.

71 LAKESIDE DINING HALL, PALMER LAKE

Lakeside Dining Hall, located at the east end of Palmer Lake between the Ridgecrest and Lakeside Residential communities, was designed by Davis Architects from Birmingham and opened in 2007 to meet the needs of the thousands of students now living on the north side of campus. Older alumni will remember Palmer Lake as the "Fishing Lake," a once secluded body of

Lakeside Dining Hall,
Palmer Lake

water visible from the rear windows of Somerville, Palmer, and (now demolished) Mallet, and McCorvey dormitories.

72 TUTWILER HALL

Tutwiler Hall was completed in 1968 to replace the original Tutwiler Hall
[22], demolished to build the Rose Administration Building [35], and was
originally planned to be the first of four high-rise dormitories. It was designed by Lawrence Whitten and Son, Birmingham architects who, earlier
in the decade, had designed Mary Burke and Martha Parham halls [33]. This
thirteen-story, 975-bed structure, like so much of 1960s Modernist architecture, ignored its domestically scaled surroundings and towers over the
southern portion of campus.

"A palace," gushed a reporter for the *Tuscaloosa News* at Tutwiler's
opening on August 7, 1968. After describing the decor of the main floor, the
writer noted that the director of women's housing and the dean of women
had designed the foyers in all twelve upper floors in different colors and furniture styles, including Early American, Danish Modern, Italian, and French
Provincial. Its small, double occupancy rooms contained custom designed,

Tutwiler Hall

built-in furniture. A semester before the dorm opened, a former typing room in Mary Burke East had been outfitted with the new furniture, and two coeds agreed to room there to test its serviceability. Their predictable complaint was lack of closet space. In Tutwiler, however, storage rooms for luggage were provided as well as "a formal room with rods designed extra high to hold the necessary evening gowns which are a part of every co-ed's life."

BRYCE CAMPUS TOUR

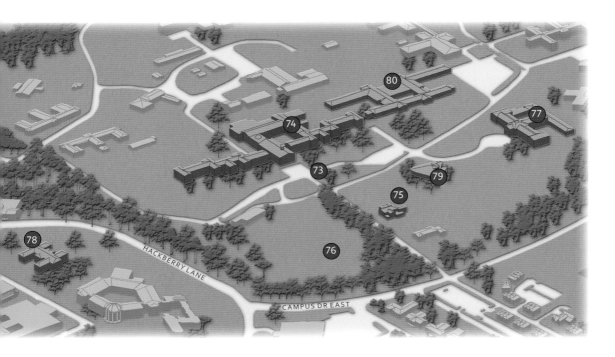

73 Bryce Hospital

74 Kirkbride Building

75 Superintendent's Mansion

76 Bryce Graves

77 Women's Reception Building

78 James B. McMillan Building

79 Bryant-Jordan Chapel

80 Bryce Admissions Building

73 BRYCE HOSPITAL

In 2010 the University of Alabama purchased the remaining portions of the grounds of Bryce Hospital, thus increasing the size of the campus by over one-third. (For information on the university's earlier purchases of portions of hospital property see "The Bryce Hospital Land Swap," p. 28, and "2010 Bryce Hospital Purchase," p. 32.) The history of this venerable neighbor of the Capstone is as remarkable in its own right as that of the university. The following tour of selected sites and buildings is designed to acquaint visitors with that institution's history. The absorption of its physical facilities and historic landscape into the university's master plan presents both challenges and exciting opportunities to preserve and interpret an important part of Alabama's social and architectural history.

The original Alabama Insane Hospital building [74] was designed to house 250 patients in a pastoral setting of 326 acres. A century after the hospital's construction the institution now known as Bryce Hospital had become a virtual city of over 5,275 patients who were housed in the original building, now extended by thousands of feet of labyrinth-like additional wings on either side, and in numerous adjacent structures built on the grounds. Unfortunately, due to lack of funds and overcrowding the hospital had lost its considerable nineteenth-century reputation and had become a warehouse for incarcerating the state's mentally challenged citizens. This dismal situation brought about a landmark civil rights lawsuit, *Wyatt v.*

Aerial view of Bryce Hospital, ca. 1950s

Stickney, filed in 1971, that kept Alabama's mental health system under federal court control for over thirty-three years and ultimately transformed the way people with mental disabilities are treated, not only in Alabama, but across the United States.

74 KIRKBRIDE BUILDING

Bryce Hospital's history encapsulates the architectural evolution of mental health in the United States. The main edifice, now often referred to as the Kirkbride Building, is the earliest and finest intact expression of a mid-nineteenth-century moral treatment mental hospital. Constructed between 1852 and 1861, it was one of the first such institutions physically to embody the

Kirkbride Building,
Bryce Hospital

advanced ideas of hospitalization and treatment of the insane Dr. Thomas Story Kirkbride developed. One of the founders of what is now known as the American Psychiatric Association, and superintendent of the Pennsylvania Hospital for the Insane in Philadelphia, Dr. Kirkbride was America's foremost nineteenth-century authority on "moral treatment," a reform movement in psychiatry that utilized architectural design and pastoral settings as essential components in the treatment of mental illness. The building's signature configuration—a central pavilion flanked by three sets of stepped-back wings on either side—reflects the structured and carefully planned regimen of patient therapy.

The unusual structure was designed by Samuel Sloan from Philadelphia, one of the country's leading mid-nineteenth-century architects. Sloan gave architectural expression to Kirkbride's ideas about moral treatment, and the Alabama building, designed in the Italianate style, established him as the country's premier asylum architect. Innovations in mechanical equipment and fixtures these men invented included new types of doors and windows, advanced indoor plumbing, central heating, and even an early form of air conditioning. Bryce Hospital influenced scores of other hospitals both in this country and abroad due to the fact that Dr. Kirkbride used the "Alabama Plan" to illustrate his 1854 book, *On the Construction, Organization,*

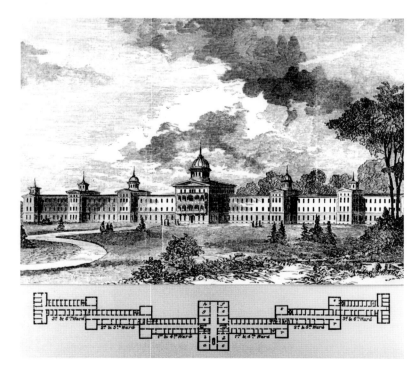

The Alabama Insane Hospital, ca. 1870, and architect's plan, 1852

and General Arrangements of Hospitals for the Insane, which went through many editions over the next forty years.

The hospital's stucco-clad brick walls were originally tinted a light pinkish tan color to imitate sandstone, and its hundreds of feet of metal roof and its massive dome were painted a deep red. In 1884 Dr. Peter Bryce, the hospital superintendent, removed the original cast iron porch from the center of the building and replaced it with the present monumental portico with its colossal columns. A few years later Dr. Bryce purchased from J. W. Fiske & Co. of New York the zinc statue of Hebe, cupbearer of the gods, that now adorns the fountain before the front entrance.

Unlike the university to its west, the Alabama Insane Hospital was not destroyed during the Federal raid on Tuscaloosa. It had played a minor role in the war effort in 1864 when its still unfinished east wings were put to use as a military hospital. Later, according to legend, local citizens, realizing that the Yankees would not likely be so inhumane as to burn down a hospital, hid their money and other valuables in the cellars below the partly occupied wings of the building. On the morning of April 4, 1865, Dr. and Mrs. Bryce, along with members of the Garland family, climbed the stairs to the dome and watched clouds of smoke rise from torched buildings in town and at the university. Later in the day Union soldiers entered the hospital grounds but did not search the building. However, they did confiscate all the horses and mules, a serious loss that deprived the hospital of animals needed for farmwork. The state government had provided little financial support during the war years and the hospital had become virtually self-sustaining.

75 SUPERINTENDENT'S MANSION

In April 1892, the hospital trustees set aside $10,000 from the "improvement fund" to build a superintendent's house on the lawn in front of the hospital. In the original Kirkbride plan, the superintendent and his family, as well as the doctors and nurses, occupied the upper floors of the central section of the main building. Patients, segregated by sex and by degrees of illness, were housed in the three adjoining wings on either side. Architect George F. Hammond from Cleveland, Ohio, designed the residence, which was constructed by Bryce patients who were supervised by hospital employees. Dr. Bryce died before the foundations were laid, and Dr. James T. Searcy took over as superintendent and completed the mansion. On February 26, 1911, fire severely damaged the building. It would have been totally destroyed if quick-thinking university students had not formed a bucket brigade.

Erection of the present house began immediately on the foundations of the old one, and the resulting structure is an eclectic blend of the remnants of the old Victorian house with naive, but charming, Classical Revival details.

Superintendent's Mansion

76 BRYCE GRAVES

A simple stone obelisk marks the grave of Dr. Peter Bryce, who served as the first superintendent of the Alabama Insane Hospital. He is buried on the grounds of the institution to which he devoted his entire career. His wife, Ellen Peter-Bryce (who, after his death, honored his memory by the now-no-longer-used custom of hyphenating her husband's first and last names), is buried beside him. Their graves are located on what was once the left front lawn of the hospital. Following the dictates of the moral treatment philosophy, the grounds of the institution were beautifully landscaped with trees, shrubs, and flowers to create a soothing and restful setting for the enjoyment of patients. Many of the magnificent magnolias were planted by Mrs. Bryce, who is also credited with having planted the unusual pistachio tree (*Pistacia chinensis*) near her husband's grave. The tree is listed in the Alabama Forestry Commission's Champion Tree program, which records the largest specimens of trees located in the state.

Over 4,500 patients who died while receiving treatment at the hospital are also buried on the property. Their graves are located in the old cemetery (earliest recorded burial 1861) located northeast of the hospital building and now bisected by the Jack Warner Parkway, and in two later cemeteries

Bryce Graves

that are located on Bryce property east of McFarland Boulevard. The earliest patient graves were, according to custom at mental institutions, marked with numbered iron (later concrete) markers—most of which have been destroyed over the years by vandalism and neglect. Today historical markers identify the sites of these cemeteries. A large granite memorial dedicated to the memory of all patients buried at the hospital was erected in 2013 in the portion of the old cemetery located south of the Jack Warner Parkway. Inscribed on it is a moving poem dedicated to these patients by the state's poet laureate.

77 WOMEN'S RECEPTION BUILDING

The Women's Reception Building, constructed in 1939 by the Birmingham architectural firm Warren, Knight, and Davis, was made possible by PWA funds. Designed in a Classical Revival style with a central Tuscan Doric Portico and surmounted by a cupola, the building was aligned on the east lawn of the main hospital to face the Male Psychiatric Building (demolished to make way for Shelby Hall) across the hospital avenue on the west.

Above: Women's Reception Building

Left: James B. Mc-Millan Building

78 JAMES B. MCMILLAN BUILDING

Named after its founding director, James B. McMillan, the structure houses the University of Alabama Press, which was established in 1945 by President Raymond Paty to operate as an academic unit of the university, its imprint controlled by a faculty University Press Committee. The only academic publisher in the state, the press publishes between eighty and ninety books a year and has a backlist of approximately 1,350 titles. Subjects include archaeology, public administration, and several areas of literature and history.

The press publishes books in a variety of formats using print, electronic, and on-demand technologies.

The McMillan Building, formerly known as Ward 34 West, was built in 1956 by Warren, Knight, and Davis Architects to house male geriatric patients. For recreation the elderly occupants, many with farming backgrounds, created a garden behind the building that, according to news accounts, soon became a source of interest and enjoyment for the staff as well as patients. In 1974 the hospital director shifted these patients to another location and used Ward 34 West for forensic patients with criminal backgrounds who had to be kept in secure surroundings.

79 BRYANT-JORDAN CHAPEL

Looking like a gigantic piece of origami, the Bryant-Jordan Interfaith Chapel designed by Davis, Speake Associates of Birmingham was dedicated in 1972. This structure and the Lurleen Wallace Chapel (demolished) at nearby Partlow State School (closed 2011) were built from the proceeds of a statewide fund drive begun in the mid-1960s. The cochairmen of the campaign were University of Alabama coach Paul "Bear" Bryant and Auburn University coach James Ralph "Shug" Jordan. Typical of Modernist church architecture of the 1960s and 1970s, the architects abandoned all references to traditional religious architecture and experimented with bold geometrical shapes and volumes.

Bryant-Jordan Chapel

80 BRYCE ADMISSIONS BUILDING

Completion of the Admissions Building in 1995 allowed hospital administrators to remove the last remaining patient wards located in the historic main Kirkbride Building. It was designed to accommodate all new patients entering the hospital. While their individual cases were being studied they were housed in the building's short-term facility for up to sixty days, after which time they were released back to their communities. Those patients needing longer stays at Bryce were housed in the extended care center where they continued to receive treatment. The design of the new structure, built by Gresham, Smith, and Partners, and Barganier Davis Sims Associated Architects of Montgomery, reflects a Postmodern interpretation of the picturesque Italianate style of the original hospital.

Bryce Admissions
Building

MEDICAL CAMPUS TOUR

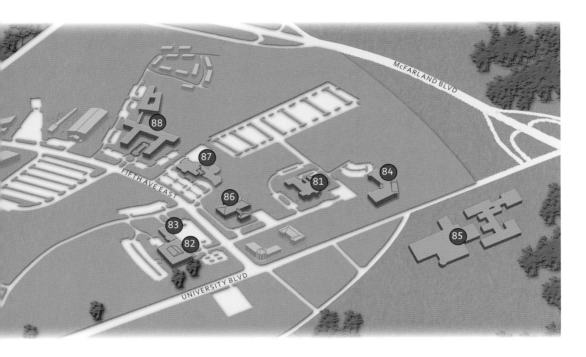

81	Speech and Hearing Center
82	University Medical Center
83	Student Health Center
84	Capstone College of Nursing
85	DCH Regional Medical Center
86	Stallings Center (RISE)
87	Child Development Research Center
88	Capstone Retirement Village

81 SPEECH AND HEARING CENTER

As early as 1971 the university determined to use portions of farmlands it had acquired from Bryce Hospital in a land swap to develop a medical campus near DCH Regional Medical Center [85].

The Department of Communicative Disorders is currently located in the former home of the University Medical Center. The department operates the Speech and Hearing Center, which offers the services of experienced, licensed, and nationally certified pathologists and audiologists who direct and supervise students in diagnostic and rehabilitative procedures.

The building, designed in a modern style by Charles H. McCauley Associates of Birmingham, is representative of the antiurban planning of the early 1970s and is notable for having no exterior windows, rendering it uninvitingly grim and tomb-like. However, the interior is surprisingly pleasant for there are interior courtyards.

82 UNIVERSITY MEDICAL CENTER

The University of Alabama Medical Center is part of the College of Community Health Sciences established in 1972 as a branch campus to the University of Alabama School of Medicine located in Birmingham. Third- and fourth-year medical students interested in family practice are provided with medical education and residency training at the center. One of the major missions of this program is to improve the health care in rural areas of Alabama, and it places an emphasis on primary health care, family medicine, and community medicine.

The center was originally located across the street in what is now the Speech and Hearing Center [81]. The new building, which opened in 2004, offers multispecialty health care to the west Alabama area, including self-contained clinics for pediatrics, internal medicine, obstetrics and gynecology, occupational health, psychiatry, neurology, surgery, and family medicine.

The University Medical Center was built by the Montgomery architectural firm of Sherlock, Smith & Adams, Architects that also designed the nearby Recreation Center. The building is yet another essay in Postmodern that incorporates classical elements. Here handsome Corinthian columns with no structural function or logic "decorate," rather incongruously, the east and west sides of this sprawling mall-like building that is bisected by two enormous overscale barrel vaulted corridors.

Fom Top:

Speech and Hearing
Center

University Medical
Center

Student Health
Center

83 STUDENT HEALTH CENTER

Adjacent to the Medical Center the Student Health Center shares administrative offices, lab space, and X-ray machines with that facility. Formerly located in Russell Hall [29], this structure is much larger with twice the number of examination rooms, each of which is equipped with a television and a painted wall mural featuring either a campus site or a sports theme.

Like the Medical Center, the Student Health Center was built by the Montgomery architectural firm of Sherlock, Smith & Adams, Architects.

84 CAPSTONE COLLEGE OF NURSING

The Capstone College of Nursing is actually the second nursing program to be developed at the university. The original one created by the legislature in 1950 was the first such program established in a state school. In 1969 it moved to the University of Alabama Medical Center in Birmingham. Its move exacerbated the nursing shortage in west Alabama and the university in 1975 established a new program at the Tuscaloosa campus that became known as the Capstone College of Nursing.

In the first years of the twenty-first century the college experienced phenomenal growth, and in 2008 the board of trustees approved construction of a new building located on the medical campus across from Druid City Regional Medical Center.

Early plans by the Birmingham architectural firm of TurnerBatson were predictably Postmodern in design. However, after numerous revisions and discussions with planners the architects developed a Neo-Traditional-style building that took advantage of the prominent location on the easternmost

Capstone College of Nursing

edge of the campus. Obviously inspired by the eighty-year-old Student Union (Reese Phifer Hall [40]), and the recently built Science and Engineering Complex [57], the corner entrance building forms a dramatic entrance to the university. As so often occurs in architecture, what for years had been deemed outmoded was now fashionable again. Architects of the 1920s and 1930s, trained in the Beaux-Arts tradition, whose work was scorned by Modern architects, were now being praised and their work was even being emulated in the early twenty-first century.

85 DCH REGIONAL MEDICAL CENTER

Although not a part of the university, the Capstone has had a long association with the DCH Regional Medical Center (originally known as Druid City Hospital). For many years the hospital was located on the university campus on land donated by the school. (See Russell Hall [29] and Nurses' Home [30].) By World War II, however, it was no longer large enough to meet the needs of the city and its surrounding area, and in 1946 the administrators of the hospital leased a portion of Northington General Hospital. (At the end of the war the army had sold the enormous two-thousand-bed complex to the university for $1.) This complex (now the site of University Mall on McFarland Boulevard) served as the home of DCH until 1952 when it moved to its present site, the new hospital having been designed by Birmingham architect Charles H. McCauley.

DCH Regional
Medical Center

In 1974 DCH entered a new phase, that of a teaching hospital, when the first residents of the university's College of Community Health Sci-

ences Family Practice Program began their training at the hospital. In a joint venture the university and DCH, with funding from the Department of Health, Education, and Welfare and a state medical bond issue, in 1977 built a seven-story addition to be used for classrooms, offices, and other facilities needed by the College of Community Health Sciences in its residency program. It was designed by Roberts Brothers–Anderson and Co., Inc., of Gadsden. The hospital, now a regional medical center, has continued to grow and is now the largest hospital in west Alabama.

86 STALLINGS CENTER (RISE)

The Stallings Center, designed by Tuscaloosa architect Jim Ward, was built in 1994 and named after former head football coach Gene Stallings, his wife Ruth Anne, and their family. An adjacent playground is named for his son Johnny, who benefited from the program.

Founded in 1974, the RISE (Rural Infant Stimulation Environment) Program is an early intervention program for children aged six weeks to five years who have known or suspected disabilities. Its services include physical, occupational, speech, and music therapies. The program serves as a practicum and intern site for university students.

87 CHILD DEVELOPMENT RESEARCH CENTER

The Child Development Research Center is part of the Department of Human Development and Family Studies in the College of Human Environmental Sciences. The center, which opened in 2005, contains a laboratory school for approximately 120 students aged two to five years, Child Development Resources, the Capstone Family Therapy Clinic, and the Pediatric Development Research Laboratory. Interdisciplinary in nature, the center is

Stallings Center (RISE)

Child Development
Research Center

also home to the Autism Spectrum Disorders Clinic from the Department of Psychology and the Belser-Parton Literacy Center from the College of Education.

The Birmingham firm of TurnerBatson Architects designed the center.

88 CAPSTONE RETIREMENT VILLAGE

Retirement communities located in university towns near or adjacent to campuses became popular in the last decades of the twentieth century. Several years in the planning stages, the Capstone Village, designed by FreemanWhite, Inc., architects of Charlotte, North Carolina, was constructed on land leased from the university. Its main building consists of a four-story complex with traditional detailing, including a colossal portico of Tuscan Doric columns.

Brochures the retirement village issued state the aims of this community: "Here, active and independent people can maintain their lifestyle while ageing with grace, companionship and peace of mind, as well as have access to University Continuing Education classes and programs, an array of sporting and arts events, reunions, concerts, and more."

Capstone Retirement
Village

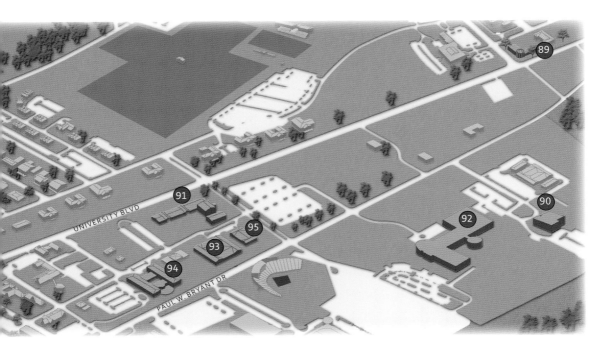

89   University of Alabama System Office: McDonald Building

90   Police Department

91   Frank M. Moody Music Building

92   Law Center

93   Paul W. Bryant Confereence Center

94   Hotel Capstone

95   Alumni Hall

89 UNIVERSITY OF ALABAMA SYSTEM OFFICE: McDONALD BUILDING

This tour begins with the new University of Alabama System Office and continues with visits to important structures located south of University Boulevard, west of DCH Regional Medical Center [85], east of Hackberry Lane, and north of the Alabama Great Southern Railroad tracks. (The Bryant Museum [96] and sports facilities in this area are included in the Athletic Campus Tour, p. 174.)

Until 1969 the university, with branch campuses in Birmingham and Huntsville and extension centers around the state, was headed by a single president located on the Tuscaloosa campus. In that year the board of trustees established separate campuses in Birmingham and Huntsville whose presidents, along with the president of the Tuscaloosa campus, reported directly to the board of trustees. In 1976 the board appointed a chancellor to oversee the operation of the three campuses and act as CEO of the system. They also mandated that he establish his office in Tuscaloosa.

The first System Office was located on Queen City Avenue (see Off Campus Tours, the Former University of Alabama System Office [106]). The new headquarters, built on campus in 2013, was named in honor of Sidney McDonald, a former president pro tem of the University of Alabama System Board of Trustees, whose generosity made possible its construction.

University of Alabama System Office Rendering

90 POLICE DEPARTMENT

Originally planned in 2007 to be located on Campus Drive on land belonging to the university behind the Publix Supermarket, the UAPD station, designed by TurnerBatson Architects, was finally built in 2011 on the other side of campus to the east of the Law School at the end of Jackson Avenue.

For over a century the university operated without a police force. That is not to say it did not need one. Like most nineteenth-century southern schools, the Capstone was a rowdy place. In the antebellum era maintaining order and discipline on campus was one of the onerous chores of the harassed and overworked faculty. Indeed, lack of discipline resulted in the resignation of the first president, Dr. Alva Woods, and his entire faculty in 1837. By the late antebellum period institution of a military form of governance did much to restore a sense of order and decorum. Nevertheless, student drunkenness, fights involving guns and knives, and altercations with townspeople remained common occurrences. Students in the first forty years of the twentieth-century, after the university was made coeducational, were better behaved, and it was only after World War II and the arrival of thousands of ex-servicemen on the GI Bill that the university administration determined to establish a campus police department in 1946, which consisted of a chief and three officers housed in a room in Woods Hall [11]. The following year the department was moved to the Student Union Building (now Reese Phifer Hall [40]). Many older alumni probably remember when it was located on University Boulevard across from Bryant-Denny Stadium in now-demolished Gorgas Hall, where it remained until 2005.

Police Department

Today the UAPD maintains a large force of full-time officers and civilian

employees whose highest priorities include maintaining the safety and well-being of students, faculty, and staff, and maintaining the security of campus.

91 FRANK M. MOODY MUSIC BUILDING

The School of Music had long outgrown its quarters in the Music and Speech Building (now Rowand-Johnson Hall [50]) when plans to erect a large new building were first envisioned. It was originally intended to be built in the northwestern section of the campus as part of the liberal arts grouping of buildings as put forward by the 1961 Greater University Development Plan. With the acquisition of land on the east side of campus in the 1970s, a new site was selected and construction was begun on the building in 1986.

The Frank Moody Music Building is named after a prominent Tuscaloosa banker and benefactor of the university. Woollen, Molzan and Partners of Indianapolis, and Fitts and White Associates of Tuscaloosa were the architects. The centerpiece of the building is a thousand-seat concert hall housing a Holtkamp organ over three stories high with sixty-five stops and over five thousand pipes.

The building was the first university structure to be built in the "Ironic Classical" variant of the Postmodern style. (See "Architectural Styles," p. 34.) Rejecting both the traditional Classical Revival used on much of the campus and the formalism of Modernism, the architects abstracted and exaggerated motifs and details borrowed from historical architectural styles and mixed them with Modernist ideas in a decidedly unorthodox manner. Such eclecticism was thought appropriate in breaking away from the strictures of Modernism. However, it was thought equally important for architects to avoid *any* suggestion of merely returning to revisionist "traditional" styles. For that reason one could borrow what one liked from the past as long

Frank M. Moody
Music Building

as one applied those borrowings in such a way that there was no mistaking them for anything but something new and of the present day.

The barnlike mass of the enormous concert hall is ornamented with pilasters of no recognizable order that ironically "support"—not an entablature, but enormous empty voids in the form of stylized semicircular windows. The main entrance to the building on the west consists of an over-scale porte cochere supported by massive concrete cylinders and covered by a gabled roof whose short end, rather than being enclosed by a classical pediment is left open to expose a massive king post truss. The north end of this part of the building terminates in a polygonal apse whose interior is illuminated by large oculi deliberately placed off center.

Abutting this part of the building and paralleling University Boulevard is a long wing featuring gables (said to be reminiscent of the Victorian Campus), abstracted, round arched windows, and a curious recessed round arched entrance that looks like an enormous culvert. Marching to the beat of a different drummer, the Moody Music Building stands out from the rest of the academic buildings on campus.

92 LAW CENTER

The massive Law Center, completed in May 1978, replaced the cramped quarters in Farrah Hall [31], which the school had long outgrown. The new building contains classrooms, seminar and conference rooms, faculty offices, a courtroom, and the major law library in Alabama, which is used by practicing attorneys throughout the state. In addition it contains the Hugo Black Room, with memorabilia of Black's career as a US senator and a justice of the US Supreme Court, his personal library, and other material relating to his life and career.

Edward Durrell Stone and Associates of New York and Pearson, Tittle, Narrows, and Associates of Montgomery, designed the Law Center. Stone, who died several months after the completion of the building, was one of America's most widely known Modern architects. Earlier in his career he had designed the Museum of Modern Art in New York and the Kennedy Center for the Performing Arts in Washington. The Law Center is entirely Modern in style, but the architects claimed that they were freely interpreting what they saw as characteristic features of southern buildings. The large glass area in the center of the facade they said was reminiscent of the dogtrot in pioneer cabins, while the massive stylized columns suggested the pillared antebellum mansions and public buildings of the South. The dramatic spiral

staircase on the interior was said to reflect the sweeping staircases of the   Law Center
President's Mansion [4] and the Gorgas House [8].

The Law School was renovated and enlarged in 2006 by KPS Group, Inc., of Birmingham and Hartman Cox of Washington, DC.

93 PAUL W. BRYANT CONFERENCE CENTER

The idea of constructing a continuing studies/alumni center was first developed in 1972. For fourteen years the original scheme underwent numerous modifications until construction of the present complex consisting of a hotel, conference center, museum, and alumni hall began in 1986. The complex dominates the northern end of Coliseum Drive.

Plans were prepared by the architectural firm of Skidmore, Owens, and Merrill. Eventually, the project was taken over by the Birmingham firm Giattina, Fisher, and Associates, and the design of the complex was considerably changed. The result was a collection of rather bland, Modernist buildings. The conference center can accommodate groups of 20 to 1,200 people in a variety of rooms, including fourteen meeting rooms.

94 HOTEL CAPSTONE

The Hotel Capstone offers convenient on-campus accommodations for visitors to the university in 150 guest rooms with large-screen televisions with premium cable service. Complimentary wireless Internet access is available in public areas. Groups and conferences are welcomed and the hotel offers on-site meeting spaces equipped with audio-visual equipment. An additional 30,000 square feet of meeting space in the adjacent Paul W. Bryant Conference Center [93] is also available. Other amenities include an outdoor

Above: Paul W. Bryant Confereence Center

Right: Hotel Capstone

pool, fitness facility, restaurant, and bar/lounge. Event catering and banquet facilities are also available. The hotel is within easy walking distance of the Quad, student religious centers, and major university cultural and athletic venues.

95 ALUMNI HALL

Alumni Hall was completed in 1987 as part of the Bryant Conference Center. It contains offices for the National Alumni Association and the offices of Alumni Affairs that were formerly located in Temple Tutwiler Hall [39]. The university has always benefited from the strong support of its alumni. Originally known as the Society of the Alumni, the organization

was rechartered in 1927 as the Alumni Association of the University of Alabama. In 2012 the association, composed of more than one hundred active
chapters with over thirty-three thousand members, awarded approximately
$4 million in scholarships.

Alumni Hall

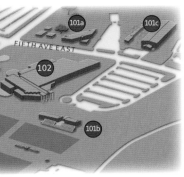

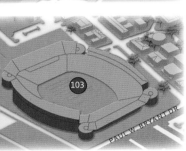

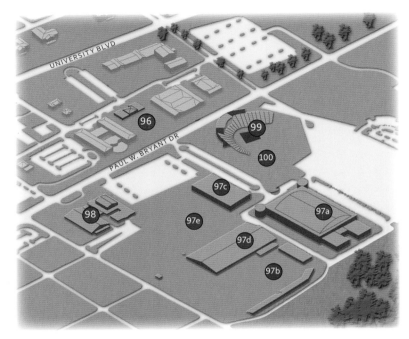

96   Bryant Museum

97a   Coleman Coliseum

97b   Sam Bailey Track and Field Stadium

97c   Mal Moore Athletic Facility

97d   Hank Crisp Indoor Practice Facility

97e   Thomas-Drew Practice Fields

98   Aquatic Center

99   Sewell-Thomas Baseball Stadium

100   Sarah Patterson Champions Plaza

101a   Rhoads Stadium

101b   Women's Soccer Stadium

101c   Roberta Alison Baumgardner Indoor Tennis Facility

102   Student Recreation Center

103   Bryant-Denny Stadium

96 BRYANT MUSEUM

The Bryant Museum, built as part of the Paul W. Bryant Conference Center [93], Hotel Capstone [94], and Alumni Hall [95] complex, features the history of football at the Capstone from 1892 to the present. It was named in honor of Coach Paul William Bryant Sr. who, during his thirty-eight-year career as a collegiate head coach, led his teams at the university to six national championships, thirteen SEC championships, and a remarkable overall record of 323-85-17. Bryant died in 1983 and was inducted posthumously into the National Football Foundation's College Football Hall of Fame in New York in December of that year.

The museum features displays enhanced by videos highlighting games, players, and coaches from the introduction of football at the university in 1892 to the present. It also contains a research library open to the public that contains a growing collection of books, journals, media guides, programs, photographs, audio and video tapes, and memorabilia. Among the more unusual artifacts housed in the museum are a Waterford crystal re-creation of Coach Bryant's famous houndstooth hat and sheets of 32-cent postage stamps depicting Coach Bryant issued in 1996 by the US Postal Service. "Namesake" day is an unusual annual event. On that day the museum invites to a reunion the over six hundred members of the public whose parents named them after the famous Crimson Tide coach.

Bryant Museum

97 COLEMAN COLISEUM

A multipurpose field house and fifteen-thousand-seat auditorium, originally called Memorial Coliseum [97a], opened on January 30, 1968, with the performance of a Broadway production, *The Roar of the Greasepaint, the Smell of the Crowd.* The structure was named in memory of university alumni who had given their lives in the service of their country in two world wars and other twentieth-century conflicts. In 1988 the building was renamed to honor Jeff Coleman, who served as the business manager of Alabama athletics from 1927 to 1954 and director of alumni affairs from 1954 to 1974.

The coliseum has been used continuously by the university's Crimson Tide basketball and gymnastics teams, but over the years it has also served as the venue for other large events. Older alumni are well acquainted with this building, having spent many hours there waiting patiently in line to sign up for classes in the era before online computer registration. Commencement exercises were moved there from Bryant-Denny Stadium [103] soon after the construction of the coliseum, and for years thousands of proud Alabama families have watched their sons and daughters walk across its temporary stage to receive their diplomas. Other historic and popular events that have occurred in this enormous structure include a 1969 sesquicentennial celebration for the city of Tuscaloosa and the state of Alabama, a speech by President Ronald Reagan, and concerts by such popular celebrities as Elvis Presley, Ray Charles, Bob Dylan, the Rolling Stones, the Grateful Dead, Hank Williams, Liza Minnelli, Reba McEntire, and Jimi Hendrix.

Coleman Coliseum

The university had begun saving funds for a field house in the late 1920s. Two such buildings reached the drawing-board stage, but construction was delayed because of higher priorities elsewhere on the campus. The present structure, whose shape is reminiscent of a colossal Quonset hut, is a modification of a design submitted in 1960 by the firm of Miller, Martin, Lewis, & McCowan of Birmingham in consultation with New York structural engineers Amman and Whitney. The original design placed the main entrance on one of the long sides of the building. When it was finally built in the late 1960s, Edwin McCowan, architect and engineer, and his associate William Paul Knight of Birmingham, moved the main entrance to the north end and prefaced it with a colonnade of stylized columns in another attempt to "relate" the building to the rest of the campus. Coleman Coliseum underwent a major renovation in 2005 undertaken by the Birmingham architectural firm of Davis Architects.

Nearby are the Sam Bailey Track and Field Stadium [97b] and three facilities associated with football: the Mal Moore Athletic Facility [97c], Hank Crisp Indoor Practice Facility [97d], and the Thomas-Drew Practice Fields [97e].

98 AQUATIC CENTER

The oldest part of the complex, the 1959 Natatorium, designed by Miller, Martin, and Lewis, occupies the northwest corner of Thomas Field. The growing national prominence of the university's swimming program in the   Aquatic Center

1970s resulted in the construction of the Olympic-sized Aquatic Center to the west of the Natatorium, designed by the architectural firm of Blondheim, Williams, and Golson, Inc., of Birmingham. Future plans call for the removal of the Aquatic Center to the northwest side of campus. Its current location will become the site of a multistory parking deck.

The Aquatic Center, home to the University of Alabama swimming and diving teams, features an Olympic-size pool and diving platforms. University Recreation offers a variety of aquatic programs, including swimming lessons for all ages and abilities, life guard training, CPR/AED training, first aid training, life guard instructor training, master's swimming, and water safety instructor training.

99 SEWELL-THOMAS BASEBALL STADIUM

The ballpark that opened in 1948 was originally named Thomas Field in honor of former football coach Frank Thomas. In 1978 it was renamed Sewell-Thomas Field in honor of former baseball coach and 1977 Hall of Fame winner Joe Sewell. The stadium, known as "the Joe" by Alabama fans, underwent major renovations by Davis Architects of Birmingham in 2010 and now has a seating capacity of over 6,500.

Although it may come as a surprise to some visitors, baseball has a longer tradition at the university than football. According to Professor Eugene Allen Smith, students first played the game on campus in 1871. In the next decade several teams were organized, including the Hiawathas, Pastimes, and Calhounians. Games were played under the Spalding rules. Smith noted

Sewell-Thomas
Baseball Stadium

that the "curved ball" was brought to the university by Adrian Vandegraaff, a Tuscaloosa native and transfer student from Yale. At that school in 1880 he had been a substitute player on Yale's first football team.

Rendering of the
Sarah Patterson
Champions Plaza

100 SARAH PATTERSON CHAMPIONS PLAZA

The Sarah Patterson Champions Plaza adjacent to Sewell-Thomas Stadium was designed by Davis Architects in 2012 as a site to provide recognition for the achievements of all university athletic programs. Plaques and memorials honor award-winning coaches and teams of all sports. The plaza was named after women's gymnastics coach Sarah Patterson, who was hired by Paul "Bear" Bryant in 1978. By 2012 Patterson's gymnastics teams had appeared in thirty consecutive NCAA National Championships and won six of them. Her squads had also won seven SEC Championships and twenty-seven NCAA regional titles.

101 SOFTBALL, SOCCER, AND TENNIS STADIUMS

Three varsity sports facilities were completed in the first five years of this century. In 2000 the architectural firm Rosser International designed the Women's Softball Stadium across from the Student Recreation Center. In 2010 it was named Rhoads Stadium [101a] in honor of John and Ann Rhoads, members of the Alumni Association who have been active supporters of women's varsity sports. In 2004 Woolpert, Inc., of Dayton, Ohio, and Almon Associates of Tuscaloosa designed the nearby Women's Soccer Stadium [101b] and the Men's and Women's Tennis Stadium. Seven years later in 2011 Ellis Architects of Tuscaloosa designed the adjacent Roberta

From Top:

Rhodes Stadium

Women's Soccer Stadium

Roberta Alison Baumgardner Tennis Facility

Alison Baumgardner Indoor Tennis Facility [101c] that houses six NCAA regulation courts. In 1963 Miss Alison was recruited to play on the University of Alabama men's tennis team. This unusual event set a precedent at the Capstone and, indeed, for the entire region, for it marked the first official move toward allowing women to participate in the Southeastern Conference of the NCAA. By 2011 there were twelve women's varsity sports on campus. The Women's Athletic Program was established in 1974 at the Capstone as an initial attempt to bring the university in compliance with Title IX of the Educational Act of 1972 that required all schools to provide gender equity in their sports programs. Four years later the program merged with the men's athletic program to assure that women would have greater equity in benefits to students.

102 STUDENT RECREATION CENTER

When the original section of the Student Recreation Center was completed in 1983, it was hailed as one of the finest in the southeast. In 1979 a committee of students, faculty, and administrators reviewed the plans of eight architectural firms and selected the one presented by Blondheim, Williams, and Golson, Inc., a Birmingham firm that also designed the Aquatic Center [98].

To meet the needs of twenty-first-century students the Rec Center was greatly enlarged by TMP Associates, Inc., and the Montgomery firm of Sherlock, Smith & Adams, Architects, and reopened in 2004. The older boxlike Modern structure is now encased in a dramatic steel, glass, and

Student Recreation Center

brick Postmodernist building that contains an extraordinary variety of facilities, including two multipurpose gyms, nine multipurpose courts, weight machines, a jogging track, climbing wall, cardio area, a four-lane indoor swimming pool, dry and steam saunas, twelve lighted tennis courts, four aerobics rooms, eight racquetball courts, a spin studio, a squash court, and locker rooms. Due to rapid increases in enrollment even this extensive expansion was insufficient to meet student needs, and plans were made in 2011 for an additional North Campus Recreation Center adjacent to the Presidential Village Residential Community [70d].

The current Student Recreation centers are far removed from the first student gymnasium located in Oliver-Barnard Hall [16]. But the current popularity of complex weight machines, spas, saunas, and physical fitness in general seems remarkably similar to the "physical culture" craze on college campuses in the last quarter of the nineteenth century, a craze that resulted in introducing physical education to the curriculum of most schools and colleges.

103 Bryant-Denny Stadium

Plans for the university's football stadium were provided by Thomas Clark Atwood and Arthur Cleveland Nash whose North Carolina architectural firm produced designs for stadiums at the University of North Carolina at Chapel Hill, Duke University, and the University of Georgia. Earlier in his career Atwood had served as the supervising engineer of the 1913 Yale Bowl. Like the Yale Bowl, the Alabama plan was based on an oval. The university did not have funds to build the entire stadium but the first section, consisting of 12,072 seats on the west side of the field, was completed in 1929 and named in honor of President George Denny. Bleacher seats were used on the east side and in the end zones until 1936, when PWA funds made possible a concrete section seating 6,000, which was erected on the east. By 1950 the stadium had been enlarged by the architects, Miller, Martin, and Lewis, to 30,000 seats, and by 1966 the bowl design had been completed. Rather than construct an oval bowl, however, as had been originally planned, the architects flattened the ends of the oval to bring end-zone seats closer to the playing field. At that time the stadium seated 56,000 spectators. Since then the stadium has undergone many renovations and enlargements (the latest by Davis Architects of Birmingham) and by 2010 the gargantuan structure had a seating capacity of 10l,821, making it one of the largest stadiums in the country.

In 1975 the stadium was renamed Bryant-Denny Stadium to honor famed Alabama coach Paul W. "Bear" Bryant. Many of his outstanding achievements were accomplished in this stadium. Here, under his direction, the Crimson Tide won seventy-two games out of seventy-four, including fifty-seven consecutive victories between October 26, 1963, and November 13, 1982. Bryant's teams never lost a homecoming game in his twenty-five years at the university.

The north side of the stadium is prefaced by a plaza referred to as the "Walk of Champions," where on game days players disembark from buses on University Boulevard and walk into the stadium. The 100-yard walkway is lined with over-life-size bronze images of Alabama football coaches who have won national championships. Also located there are markers commemorating the Crimson Tide's National Championships and Southeastern Conference Championships.

Left: View of Bryant-Denny Stadium from the southeast

Below: Bryant-Denny Stadium, North Front

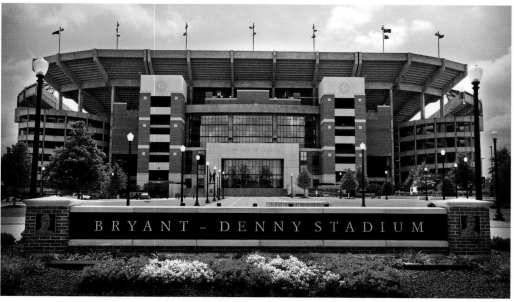

TOUR 12   OFF CAMPUS TOURS

104   Park at Manderson's Landing

105   The University Club

106   Former University System Office

107   Former Chancellor's Home

108   Arboretum

109   Brewer-Porch Children's Center

110   Moundville Archeological Park, Moundville, Alabama

111   Tanglewood, J. Nicholene Bishop Biological Station

104 PARK AT MANDERSON'S LANDING

The Park at Manderson's Landing shows how valuable long-range planning can be, for the planners of the Greater University first envisioned this beautiful location as a recreational area in 1906. They proposed that the northern portion of campus adjoining the Black Warrior River should be a park for watching varsity boating crews on the river. Unfortunately, this idea was not developed and later administrations used the area as a convenient dumping ground, as well as a storage and maintenance area. Throughout much of the twentieth century most students and faculty were unaware of the proximity of the river. The dump was finally removed in the late 1960s, only to be replaced by River Road (now the Jack Warner Parkway) with its four lanes of traffic that separate the campus from the riverbank.

But after more than a century a riverside park has been realized with the creation of the Park at Manderson's Landing located along the river's edge. It connects to the west with a municipal park creating a narrow, but attractive series of walking and biking trails with unexcelled views of river activity, which include commercial barges, pleasure boats, triathlon events, and varsity boating crews. The park was named in honor of Atlanta businessman Lewis M. Manderson and his wife, Faye, who made generous donations to the university's "Our Students, Our Future" campaign.

Park at Manderson's Landing

105 THE UNIVERSITY CLUB

In 1946 the H. D. Warner family assisted the university in acquiring the antebellum James H. Dearing House (circa 1834) on Queen City Avenue and University Boulevard for a dining club for faculty and staff (membership is also available to the general public). For over sixty-five years the Warner family has generously supported the facility financially and with donations of fine period furnishings and works of art.

The University Club has many associations with the Capstone. It was probably designed by architect William Nichols, and it was certainly built by skilled carpenters, bricklayers, and stonemasons who had earlier worked with him on the capitol and university buildings. The residence's original owner, James H. Dearing, was a pioneer of Tuscaloosa who had become wealthy as a steamboat captain and merchant. His new house was the first private dwelling in this area to have a large portico with two-story stuccoed brick and stone Ionic columns, and it set the fashion for numerous others during the "Flush Times" of the 1830s. Dearing lived in the house for only two years, however. He complained in the local paper that "night after night, week after week . . . companies of [university] students came by [the house on the way to and from town] . . . singing songs, most obscene, and using language that was most disgraceful and offensive to decency." Matters came to a head when students abducted one of his female slaves and took her back

The University Club

to campus. Dearing went out to the university, searched for her, and caused a near riot. In retaliation the students destroyed Dearing's front gate and raided his henhouse. Shots were fired and a student injured. Soon afterward Dearing sold the house and built a larger one in another location. Later the structure was sold to Arthur P. Bagby, who resided there while serving as governor. For this reason it is sometimes referred to as the Governor's Mansion even though it was a private house, since the state did not provide an official residence for the governor at that time. The house was later owned by Henderson M. Somerville. Judge Somerville was the founder of the University of Alabama Law School and a judge of the Alabama Supreme Court.

106 FORMER UNIVERSITY SYSTEM OFFICE

The Office of the University of Alabama System was moved to its new location on campus (see the University of Alabama System Office [89]) and the old structure was deeded to the university.

The original University of Alabama System Office was built in 1975 on a lot adjacent to the University Club [105] by Birmingham architect Henry Sprott Long, renowned for his designs of traditional-styled Mountain Brook mansions. In order to make the office building blend in with its residential surroundings, the architect kept the building domestic in scale. He also referenced the architecture of William Nichols (designer of the original

Former University System Office

1828–31 campus [see fig. 1]) in details such as the Ionic portico and elaborate fanlight over the entrance, which are based on Nichols's extant North Carolina buildings. A decade earlier, Long had used another Nichols building, the Gorgas House [8], as inspiration for his design for the Phi Gamma Delta fraternity house on University Boulevard.

107 FORMER CHANCELLOR'S HOME

In 1976 the board of trustees mandated that the newly appointed chancellor of the system live in Tuscaloosa. Fortunately, the university owned a fine house located at 9 Pinehurst, Tuscaloosa's first subdivision and only a few blocks away from campus. In 1954 Mr. and Mrs. H. D. Warner had given their house to the university with the understanding that they would continue to occupy it as long as they lived. (They had earlier donated the adjacent house on the left to the university.) Warner died in 1975 and the university had begun to refurbish it, but it was not finished when Dr. Volker became chancellor. Renovation proved costly, and for the next five years the chancellor when in Tuscaloosa lived in another university-owned residence in the Highlands. In 1980 the Warners' son, Jack, and his wife, Elizabeth, generously contributed to the restoration of the Chancellor's House, and even donated their former home located to the right of it, to the university.

Former Chancellor's Home

Two of these houses had been built in the early twentieth century by uni-

versity professors. The Chancellor's House had been built in 1907 by Dr. Edgar Kay, dean of the School of Engineering. Professor Charles Barnwell, dean of the College of Arts and Sciences, built number ll Pinehurst, now the Chancellor's Guest House. Frank Blair, a wealthy businessman, built number 7.

108 ARBORETUM

The 60-acre Arboretum, created in 1956 by a group of professors and administrators, and now a part of the University of Alabama Museums, is located near the intersection of Veterans' Memorial Parkway and Pelham Loop Road. Visitors are able to view examples of the state's native flora and fauna along two and a half miles of walking trails. Plants from Alabama's various ecological zones are represented along with rare, threatened, and endangered specimens. There is also a bog garden, a children's garden, and a wildflower garden with over 250 species. The Arboretum is open seven days a week from 8 A.M. to sunset.

109 BREWER-PORCH CHILDREN'S CENTER

Located on 60 acres near the Tuscaloosa Veterans Hospital, the Brewer-Porch Children's Center, created in 1970 by an act of the legislature and operated by the university's College of Arts and Sciences, provides a model

Arboretum

program for the state's special needs children, adolescents, and their families. It also provides experiences for university students in the area of childhood emotional disorders, autism, and mental illnesses.

The center, designed in 2006 by Williams Blackstock, Architects, of Birmingham, was named to honor Governor Albert Brewer and Representative Ralph Porch, an Alabama legislator.

110 MOUNDVILLE ARCHAEOLOGICAL PARK, MOUND-VILLE, ALABAMA

Moundville Archaeological Park, a National Historic Landmark, located 13 miles south of I20/59 on Highway 69 South and administered by the University of Alabama Museums, is one of the largest and best-preserved prehistoric Native American sites in the United States. The park, on the banks of the Black Warrior River, includes twenty-nine earthen mounds arranged around an open plaza, a museum, archaeological research center, nature trail, and camping facilities.

The university purchased the Moundville site in the early 1930s due to the untiring efforts of Dr. Walter B. Jones, a young geologist who had succeeded Dr. Eugene Allen Smith as director of the Alabama Museum of Natural History. In those Depression years money was scarce, and Dr. Jones at one point even mortgaged his own home to raise cash to purchase additional property at Moundville. Beginning in 1934 Jones employed two hundred Civilian Conservation Corps (CCC) workers who made possible large-scale excavations of the site, and the construction of the present Jones Archaeological Museum, which opened in 1939. The poured concrete Art Moderne–style museum was designed by J. T. Mitchell, Richard Nash, and Raymond Sizemore of the National Park Service. On the exterior the

Moundville Archaeo-
logical Park

central block was embellished with a frieze of alternating skull and forearm designs found on Moundville pottery. The museum originally contained in situ burials in two wings flanking a central gallery where excavated artifacts were displayed. In the 1990s due to protests from Native Americans and the passage of NAGPRA (Native American Graves Protection and Repatriation Act) the burials were closed. Today, after major renovations, the museum's galleries feature artifacts and theatrical, high-tech, Disney-like displays of imagined life (including a wedding) of the prehistoric mound builders.

111 TANGLEWOOD, J. NICHOLENE BISHOP BIOLOGICAL STATION

Located near Akron in Hale County, the J. Nicholene Bishop Biological Station consists of an 1859 Greek Revival house (recorded by the Historic American Buildings Survey) and a 480-acre plantation purchased by Page Harris in 1824. The property was donated to the university in 1949 by Harris's great-granddaughter with the stipulation that it be named to honor her aunt, J. Nicholene Bishop, who had attended the Alabama Normal College in Livingston (now West Alabama University). Later (thanks to her long friendship with Julia Tutwiler), she became one of the first ten female resident students to attend the University of Alabama. Julia Tutwiler's childhood home and site of her father's famous school, Green Springs Academy, was located near Tanglewood, and Julia was a frequent visitor there. If you are visiting Tanglewood be sure to stop at the Havana Methodist Church Cemetery and view the graves of Julia and her father, Henry, who was one of the original faculty members of the University of Alabama.

For over sixty years Tanglewood has served as a plant and wildlife sanctuary, and the university now uses it to assist in undergraduate and graduate research in biodiversity and environmental processes. In 2010 the university built a pavilion on the site, designed by Summerour and Associates, Architects, Inc., that features a classroom with stone fireplace and a lab/kitchen area for use during inclement weather and for use by students for the study of samples collected at the station. It also functions as a staging area for field instruction for learning to use, maintain, and house land management equipment, and includes secure storage for supplies.

Tanglewood, J. Nicho-
lene Bishop Biological
Station

Glossary

ABACUS The top portion of a column capital, on which the entablature, or object supported, rests. The square topmost member of a Doric or Tuscan Doric column.

ACROTERIA Roof ornaments at the peak or ends of a classical pediment.

ADAMESQUE A building or object in the manner of the classically derived style of the Adam brothers (English, eighteenth century).

AMERICAN BOND OR COMMON BOND A brickwork bond composed of either three or five courses of stretchers (the long side of bricks) to each course of headers (the short ends of bricks).

APSE A semicircular or polygonal structure, which is seen as a recess inside a building and as a projection outside.

ARCADE A series of arches supported by columns or piers.

ARCH A curved, sometimes pointed structural member used to span an opening. Arches are often classified either by historical criteria (e.g., Gothic arch) or according to the curve of the arch (e.g., segmented arch).

ARCHITRAVE The lowest part of a classical entablature resting directly on the capital columns or piers and supporting the frieze and cornice.

ASHLAR Squared stone characterized by a high quality finish and thin mortar joints.

ATTIC In classical architecture, the space above the entablature or wall cornice. On Roman triumphal arches, a place for inscriptions.

BALUSTRADE A railing system used along the edge of balconies, porches, stairs, terraces, and roofs composed of a series of balusters supporting a rail or coping.

BARREL VAULT A masonry vault resting on two parallel walls and having the form of a half cylinder.

BATTLEMENT See Crenellation.

BAY Any of a series of major divisions or units in a structure, as window, door, or archway, openings, or the space between columns or piers.

BLIND ARCADE Arches within a wall framing a recessed flat panel rather than an opening; used to enliven an otherwise plain expanse of masonry or to decrease the dead weight of the wall.

BONDING The term *bonding* refers to the repeating arrangement of bricks into various patterns.

BUTTRESS A pier built into or against a wall to help it resist lateral forces.

CAMPANILE A bell tower, usually freestanding.

CAPITAL The upper decorated portion of a column or pilaster on which the entablature rests.

COLONNADE A series of regularly spaced columns; an open passageway with columns.

COLOSSAL COLUMN A column that reaches more than one story in height.

COLUMN A pillar, usually circular in plan. The parts of a column in classical architecture are base, shaft, and capital.

COMPOSITE ORDER A Roman order with a distinctive capital that combines the acanthus leaf employed on the Corinthian order with the volutes of the Ionic order.

CORINTHIAN ORDER The most ornate of the Greek orders, characterized by a bell-shaped capital embellished with acanthus leaves.

CORNICE In classical architecture the topmost projecting part of an entablature, resting on the frieze and composing the base of the pediment.

CRENELLATION Any decorative element that simulates the squares (merlons) and the spaces (embrasures, crenels) of a defensive parapet.

CRESTING The ornamental finish at the ridge of a roof.

CUPOLA A rounded, towerlike device rising from the roof of a classical building typically terminating in a miniature dome.

DENTICULATED See Dentil.

DENTIL A small rectangular toothlike block used in a series below the cornice in some classical orders.

DISTYLE-IN-ANTIS In classical architecture a portico with two columns set between the piers (antae) of the flanking walls.

DORIC See Order.

English bond A bond composed of alternating courses of stretchers and headers. (Note that the bricks in all stretcher courses line up vertically.)

Entablature In classical architecture, the part of a building carried by the columns. It consists of a cornice, frieze, and architrave.

Entasis In classical architecture, the subtle convex curve of the shaft of a column used in order to correct the optical illusion of concavity that would result from a straight-sided column.

Facade The face of a building, especially the principal face as front.

Finial An ornament that caps a gable, hip, pinnacle, or other architectural feature.

Flemish bond Headers and stretchers alternate in each course with the center of each header over the center of the stretcher directly below it.

Fluting Vertical, concave channels on columns, pilasters, and other surfaces.

Frieze The central part of the entablature between the architrave below and the cornice above.

Greek Doric The oldest and simplest of the Greek orders, with a simple rounded column capital, no base, and properly an entablature with a frieze composed of triglyphs and metopes.

Header See Bonding.

Hexastyle A classical portico having six columns.

Hood mold The projecting molding over a door or window that extends horizontally over a square opening and vertically downward a short distance, parallel to either side of the opening.

Ionic order A Greek order characterized by its elaborate scroll-like capital composed of volutes.

King post The vertical post from the tie beam to the apex of a triangular truss.

Lyceum A hall for public lectures or discussions.

MANSARD A roof having short, steep slopes on four sides, with a much shallower pitched, or nearly flat, platform-like roof above.

MODULE A unit of measurement governing the proportions of a building. In classical architecture the module was either the diameter or half the diameter of a column at the base of the shaft. In modern architecture the module is any unit of measurement devised by architects, usually to facilitate prefabrication.

OBELISK A tall, narrow, square shaft, tapering and ending in a pyramidal point.

OCULUS (Latin, "eye"), a circular window in a wall or at the apex of a dome.

ORDER Any of several types of classical columns, including pedestal and bases and entablatures. The Greeks developed Doric, Ionic, and Corinthian. The Romans added Tuscan Doric and Composite, which merged the features of the Ionic and Corinthian.

PALLADIAN WINDOW A window composed of a central arched sash flanked on either side by smaller rectangular side lights.

PARAPET A low wall or protective railing often used along the edge of a roof.

PEDIMENT The triangular gable above the entablature of a classical temple enclosed by the horizontal cornice of the entablature and raking cornices following the edges of the roof.

PILASTER A rectangular column or shallow pier attached to a wall frequently treated to represent a classical column.

POLYCHROMY In architecture, the use of many building materials of contrasting colors.

PORTE COCHERE A covered entrance, or porch, projecting far enough across a driveway or entrance road so that automobiles or other wheeled vehicles may pass through.

QUOINS Large stones, or rectangular pieces of wood or brick, used to decorate and accentuate the corners of a building; laid in vertical series with, usually, alternately large and small blocks.

ROMAN IONIC A variation of the classical Ionic order used by the Romans. The capitals of columns have angle volutes, thus showing the scroll on all four sides.

Rotunda A circular building or room, usually domed.

Roundel A circular panel, window, or niche.

String course A continuous band of brick, stone, or wood on the exterior wall of a building used for decorative purposes, or as a means of breaking up a large expanse of wall surface.

Tower of the winds order A variation on the Corinthian order.

Tuscan (Roman) Doric order A Roman order derived from the Greek Doric but slimmer, of greater simplicity, with a base, unfluted column shaft, and simple capital.

Truss Essentially a triangle formed by any one of a combination of structural members into a rigid roof framework for spanning between two load-bearing walls.

Veneer A decorative layer of brick, wood, or other material used to cover inferior structural material, thereby giving an improved appearance at a low cost.

Suggested Reading

Byrd, Gene. "F. A. P. Barnard and Astronomy in the Antebellum South." *Alabama Heritage* 15 (Spring 2000): 17–25.

Byrd, Gene, and Robert Mellown. "An Antebellum Observatory in Alabama." *Sky and Telescope* 65 (February 1983): 113–15.

———. "F. A. P. Barnard and Alabama's First Observatory." *Journal of the Alabama Academy of Science* 57 (January 1986): 39–44.

Center, Clark E., Jr. "The Burning of the University of Alabama." *Alabama Heritage* 5 (Spring 1990): 30–45.

Clark, Willis G. *History of Education in Alabama, 1702–1889.* Washington, DC: US Government Printing Office, 1889.

Hall, John. "Capsule in a Cornerstone: The Treasure of Smith Hall." *Alabama Heritage* 25 (Fall 2010): 18–24.

Hoole, William Stanley, and Elizabeth Hoole McArthur. *The Yankee Invasion of West Alabama, March–April 1865.* Tuscaloosa: Confederate Publishing Company, 1985.

Hubbs, G. Ward. "'Dissipating the Clouds of Ignorance': The First University of Alabama Library, 1831–1865." *Libraries and Culture* 27 (Winter 1992): 20–35.

Hughes, Delos D. "Jefferson's 'Academical Village.'" *Alabama Heritage* 12 (Spring 1997): 22–31.

Mathews, Mary Chapman. *A Mansion's Memories.* Tuscaloosa: University of Alabama Press, 2006.

Mellown, Robert O. "The Alabama Rotunda." *Alabama Heritage* 12 (Spring 1997): 32–37.

———. "The Construction of the Alabama Insane Hospital, 1852–1861." *Alabama Review* 38 (April 1985): 83–104.

———. "Mental Health and Moral Architecture." *Alabama Heritage* 9 (Spring 1994): 5–17.

———. "Nichols in Alabama: Lost Treasures." *Society for the Fine Arts Review* 4 (Summer 1982): 7–9.

———. "The President's Mansion at the University of Alabama." *Alabama Review* 35 (July 1982): 200–229.

———. "A Stained-Glass Tiffany Knight." *Alabama Heritage* 8 (Winter 1993): 44–45.

———. *The University of Alabama: A Guide to the Campus.* Tuscaloosa: University of Alabama Press, 1988.

———. "The University of Alabama: An Architectural History of the Old Quad." Part 1. *Society for the Fine Arts Review* 6 (Fall 1984): 12–15.

———. "The University of Alabama: An Architectural History of the Old Quad." Part 2. *Society for the Fine Arts Review* 7 (Winter 1985): 13–16.

Oldshue, Jerry C. "Historical Archaeology on the University of Alabama Campus." *Alabama Review* 30 (January 1977): 266–75.

Peatross, Ford, and Robert O. Mellown. *William Nichols, Architect.* Tuscaloosa: University of Alabama Sarah Moody Art Gallery, 1979.

Sartwell, Alexander. "A Brief History of Smith Hall." *Nature South: The Magazine of the Alabama Natural History Society* 4 (1994): 3–5.

Sellers, James B. *History of the University of Alabama.* Vol. 1. Tuscaloosa: University of Alabama Press, 1953.

Schnorrenberg, John M. "Remembered Past, Discovered Future: The Alabama Architecture of Warren Knight & Davis (1906–1961)." Birmingham: Birmingham Museum of Art, 1999.

Scott, John B., Jr. "Frank Lockwood and His Architectural Legacy." *Alabama Heritage* 17 (Spring 2002): 32–41.

Shelby, Thomas Mark. *D. O. Whilldin: Alabama Architect.* Birmingham: Birmingham Historical Society, 2009.

Stern, Robert A. M. *Modern Classicism.* New York: Rizzoli, 1988.

Turner, Paul Venable. *Campus: An American Planning Tradition.* Cambridge, MA: MIT Press, 1985.

Wolfe, Suzanne Rau. *The University of Alabama: A Pictorial History.* Tuscaloosa: University of Alabama Press, 1983.

Photograph Credits

Photographs courtesy of:

Rachel Dobson: 44 (above), 59 (above), 76, 94, 97 (above), 114, 119 (below), 131, 132, 139, 147, 153, 154, 155, 157, 162, 178, 188, 190

Facilities and Planning, the University of Alabama: 127 (top), 128 (middle), 130, 138 (below), 144 (middle), 144 (bottom)

Teresa Golson: 42

Duane A. Lamb: ii, 51 (above), 55, 56, 68, 70 (right), 72, 73 (above), 75 (above), 79, 90, 91, 95, 104, 107, 110, 115, 119 (above), 125, 127 (middle), 129 (top, bottom), 133, 150, 156, 161, 163, 168, 172 (above), 173, 180, 183 (left), 186, 187, 189

Robert Oliver Mellown: 38 (below), 39

Dickie Turnbull: 87, 160 (top), 177

University of Alabama Division of Financial Affairs, 96 (below), 127 (top), 129 (middle), 130, 138 (below), 144 (middle, bottom), 179

University Relations, the University of Alabama: 82, 111, 116 (below), 121, 122, 123, 124, 135, 138 (above), 140, 142, 144 (top), 169, 172 (right), 193; Chip Cooper, 48, 106, 143, 160 (middle), 164, 181; Jeffrey Hanson, 134, 165; Samantha Hernandez, 80, 109, 116 (above), 118; Bryan Hester, 61, 65, 84, 92, 108, 112, 113, 127 (bottom), 183 (below), 185; Zachary Riggins, 101, 141 (above), 171, 175; Laura Shill, 146, 160 (below), 176, 191; Frazer Spowart, 141 (below); Rickey Yanaura, 98, 117

W. S. Hoole Special Collections Library, the University of Alabama: 38 (above), 44 (right), 46 (above), 49, 51 (left), 59 (below), 70 (above), 73 (below), 75 (below), 77, 85, 97 (below), 149, 151

Index

Abercrombie, John W., 13, 14, 19, 86

"academical village," 5, 17

Adams, Herbert B., 74

Adams Hall, 107,

Agnes Ellen Harris Hall, 107

AIME Building, 31, 120, 125–26

Air Force Reserve Officers' Training Program, 74, 91

Alabama Business Hall of Fame, 114

Alabama Department of Mental Health, 32, 140

Alabama Insane Hospital. *See* Bryce Hospital

Alabama Institute for Manufacturing Excellence, 31, 120, 125–26. *See also* AIME Building

Alabama Polytechnic Institute. *See* Auburn University

Alabama State Capitol: Montgomery, 20; Tuscaloosa, 1, 3

"Album of Friendship," 6

Almon Associates, Inc., 30, 179

Alpha Tau Omega, 25

Alston, Mary Hewell, 115

Alston, Robert Nabors, 115

Alston, William W., 66

Alston Hall, 31, 102, 115–16, 128

Alumni Association. *See* University of Alabama Alumni Association

Alumni Hall, 110, 166, 171, 172–73, 175

Amelia Gayle Gorgas Library, 23, 25, 37, 41, 42, 69, 88, 89–90

American Psychiatric Association, 151

Amman and Whitney, 177

anniversary: 75th, 14, 19; 125th, 24, 26–27; 150th, 29; 175th, 139

Antebellum Campus, 1–7, 18, 36–61, 94

Aquatic Center, 174, 177–78, 181

Arboretum, 184, 189

Archaeological Classicism, 35

architectural styles, 34–35

Army Reserve Officers' Training Corps, 73

Atwood, Thomas Clark, 182

Auburn University, 25, 156

Augusta Evans Wilson Hall, 108

B. B. Comer Hall. *See* Braxton Bragg Comer Hall

Bagby, Arthur P., 187

Bakersfield, 142

Barganier Davis Sims Associated Architects, 157

Barnard, Frederick A. P., 50–51, 74, 91

Barnard Hall. *See* Oliver-Barnard Hall

Barnwell, Charles C., 108, 189

Barnwell Hall, 24, 86, 102, 108–9

Barry, Michael, 47

Bashinsky, Sloan Y., Sr., 116

Bashinsky Computer Center, 31, 35, 102, 116–17

Bath House, 23, 54

Baumgardner, Roberta Alison, 181

Beene, Jesse, 5

Benham Group, Inc., 125

Bevill, Tom, 124–25

Bevill Building, 29, 34, 120, 124–25

Bibb Graves Hall, 23, 24, 83, 102, 110, 111–12

Bidgood, Lee, 124

Bidgood Hall, 23, 69, 102, 114–15

Biology Building, 27, 34, 120, 132–33

Bishop, J. Nicholene, 192. *See also* Tanglewood

Black, Hugo, 170

Black Warrior River, 15, 26, 54, 58, 185, 190

Blackburn Institute, 110

Blair, Frank, 189

Blondheim, Williams, and Golson, Inc., 178, 181

Blount, Winton, 142

Blount Living-Learning Center, 74, 136, 142

Board of Regents, 64

Board of Trustees, 1–5, 7, 8, 11, 12, 20, 22, 30, 31, 34, 43, 47, 50, 51, 54, 58, 60, 61, 63, 64, 67, 68, 69, 71, 72, 74, 100, 105, 125, 137, 145, 161, 167, 188

Boulder, 41

Boysey (slave), 60, 61

Braxton Bragg Comer Hall. *See* Comer Hall

Brewer, Albert, 190

Brewer-Porch Children's Center, 184, 189–90

Brown, Boysey, 60, 61

Brumby, Richard T., 92

Bruno, Angelo, 116

Bruno Library, 31, 35, 102, 116–17

Bryant, Mary Harmon, 134

Bryant, Paul W. "Bear," Sr., 134, 175

Bryant Conference Center. *See* Paul W. Bryant Conference Center

Bryant Hall. *See* Paul W. Bryant Hall

Bryant Museum, 174–75

Bryant-Denny Stadium, 23, 24, 55, 103, 143, 168, 174, 176, 182–83

Bryant-Jordan Chapel, 148, 156

Bryce, Ellen Peter, 152, 153

Bryce, Peter, 50, 152, 153

Bryce Admissions Building, 148, 157

Bryce Graves, 148, 153–54

Bryce Hospital, 25, 26, 28, 29, 32, 33, 50, 60, 64, 71, 83, 85, 130, 148, 149–53, 159

Bryce Hospital Land Swap, 26, 28–29, 149

Bryce Hospital Purchase, 32, 149

Bureau of Mines. *See* ROTC Building

Burke, Mary, 100

Burke Hall. *See* Mary Burke Hall

Burwell Boykin Lewis Hall. *See* Lewis Hall

Byrd Hall. *See* Mabel Selden Byrd Hall

Cadet Laundry, 54, 62, 76–77

Campaign for Alabama, 30–31

Campus Drive Parking Deck, 131

Campus Master Plan: 1985, 30–31, 137, 139; 2007, 32, 33, 90; 2012, 33

Canonic Classicism, 35, 126

Capstone College of Nursing, 35, 97, 158, 161–62

Capstone Retirement Village, 158, 164–65

Carmichael, Oliver Cromwell, 114

Carmichael Hall, 42, 69, 102, 105, 113–14

CCC. *See* Civilian Conservation Corps

cemetery: Bryce, 148, 153–54; Evergreen, 50; University, 36, 60–61

Center for Ethics and Social Responsibility, 110

Center for the Study of Southern History and Culture, 85

Chadwick, Albert, 79

Champions Plaza. *See* Sarah Patterson Champion's Plaza

Chancellor's Home, former, 184, 188–89

Chancellor's Guest House, 189

Chapman, Mrs. Reuben, 52

Charles H. McCauley Associates, 159

Child Development Laboratory, 107–8

Child Development Research Center, 108, 128, 158, 163–64

Civilian Conservation Corps (CCC), 190

Clark, Willis G., 12, 13

Clark Hall, 9, 13, 62, 67–69, 89, 92, 103

Classical Revival Style, 1, 19, 20, 34, 58, 81, 92, 93, 95, 108, 110, 114, 126, 137, 153, 154, 169

Clayton Hall, 117

Coleman, Jeff, 176

Coleman Coliseum, 174, 176–77

College Housing Loan Program, 27

Comer, Braxton Bragg, 18, 19, 79–80, 123

Comer, Hugh Moss, 125

Comer Hall, 19, 21, 27, 46, 74, 76, 77, 78, 79–80, 119, 121, 123, 140

Confederacy, 41, 43, 57, 134

Cooke, George, 15, 16, 18, 19
Cornell Company Iron Works, 49, 56
Cowan, James Gillespie, 53, 54, 57
Crawford (slave), 58
Crawford, William J., 60
Creative Campus Initiative, 53
Crenshaw, John B., 74
Crimson Promenade, 136, 139
Crisp Indoor Practice Facility. *See* Hank Crisp
    Indoor Practice Facility
Crossland, W. A., 72

Davis, Alexander Jackson, 8–13, 58
Davis Architects, 100, 128, 129, 145, 146, 177,
    178, 179, 182
Davis, Speake Associates, 90, 156
DCH Regional Medical Center, 24, 28, 95–97,
    158, 159, 162–63, 167
Dearing, James H., 186–87
Delta Kappa Epsilon, 24
Denny, George H., 20, 22, 31, 32, 86, 89, 95,
    99, 103, 182
Denny Chimes, 102–5
Denny Field, 23, 26, 100
Denny Stadium. *See* Bryant-Denny Stadium
Design Guide, 32
Doster, James J., 106
Doster Hall, 102, 106–7
Douglas, Wilmot C., 135, 140
Dressler Hall, 137
Druid City Hospital Regional Medical Center.
    See DCH Regional Medical Center

earthworks. *See* fortifications
Ecole des Beaux Arts, 15, 16, 18, 20, 21, 90, 94,
    106, 117, 162
Ellis Architects, 179
Ellyson, Robert, 60
English Gothic Style, 8
Erosophic Literary Society, 45
Evan M. Terry Associates, 125, 130

Faraday, Michael, 92
Farrah, Albert, Jr., 99
Farrah Hall, 88, 98–99, 110, 170
Federal Raid, 7, 8, 10, 43, 44, 45, 50, 52, 53, 58,
    80, 89, 94, 152
Ferguson, Hill, 14, 18, 19, 137
Ferguson Center, 30, 34, 136–39
Fiquet, Dominique Doux, 6
Fitts and White Associates, 169
fortifications, student, 18, 36, 53–54, 57
Foster, Richard Clark, 89, 99
Foster Auditorium, 23, 26, 88, 99–100
foundations, 9, 36, 37, 39, 43, 44–47, 70, 89
fountains, 138, 152
Frank M. Moody Music Building, 28, 29, 34,
    35, 166, 169–70
Franklin Hall, 43, 44, 45, 67
FreemanWhite, Inc., 164
Freret, William, 12
Freret, William Alfred, 11–13, 49, 67, 72–73
Friedman, Hugo, 117
Friedman Hall, 102, 117, 142
Furman, Margaret Cammer, 49
Furman, Richard, 49

Gabe (slave), 58
Gallalee, John M., 94
Gallalee Hall, 24, 88, 94–95, 135
Gallaway, Marian, 119
Gallaway Theater. *See* Marian Gallaway Theater
Garikes Wilson Atkinson, Inc., 134
Garland, Landon Cabell, 5, 7, 45, 52–54, 58, 71
Garland, Mrs. Landon Cabell, 50
Garland Hall, 13, 49, 62, 71–72, 76, 89, 111
General Development Plan, 27, 123, 132
George M. Figh and Company, 64
Giattina, Fisher, and Associates, 171
Gibbs, John F., 10
Glasscock, John Henry, 6
Good & Goodstein, Inc., 141
Gordon Palmer Hall, 27, 120, 135

Gorgas, Amelia Gayle, 57, 89, 113

Gorgas, Josiah, 57, 89

Gorgas, Maria, 57

Gorgas Hall. *See* Josiah Gorgas Hall

Gorgas House, 18, 36, 55–57, 76, 91, 113, 171, 188

Gorgas Library. *See* Amelia Gayle Gorgas Library

Gothic Revival, 18, 57, 137

Gould Evans, Associates, LC, 130

Governor's Mansion: Alabama, 187; Mississippi, 3; North Carolina, 3

Governor's Palace: Virginia, 34

Graves, Bibb, 111

Graves Hall. *See* Bibb Graves Hall

Great Depression, 23, 99, 190

Greater University Campaign, 14–21

Greater University Campus, 16, 19

Greater University Committee, 14

Greater University Development Campaign, 27, 106, 123

Greater University Plan, 13, 14, 18, 20, 21, 22, 54, 79, 89, 90, 137

Green Springs Academy, 192

Gresham, Smith, and Partners, 157

Guard House, 36, 57–60

HADP Architecture, Inc., 143

Hammond, George F., 152

Hank Crisp Indoor Practice Facility, 174, 177

Hardaway, Robert A., 121

Hardaway Hall, 27, 120, 121–22

Harris, Agnes Ellen, 107

Harris, Page, 192

Harris Hall. *See* Agnes Ellen Harris Hall

Harrison, Kibble J., 66

Hartman Cox, 171

Havana Methodist Church Cemetery, 192

Hawley, Hughson, 16, 17, 18

Hayes, Marcellus T., 74

HBRA Architects, 35

HES Design House, 102, 107–8

Henderson M. Somerville Hall, 146

Henry D. Clayton Hall. *See* Clayton Hall

High Victorian Gothic, 7–13, 18, 21, 25, 49, 62–77, 139–40, 142, 152, 170

H. M. Comer Hall. *See* Mineral Industries Building

HOK, Inc., 126

Hood, James A., 100

Horne, J.T., 97

Hotel Capstone, 166, 171–72, 175

Houser, Shaler C., 122

Houser Hall, 24, 27, 120, 122

Howard College, 11

Hugh Moss Comer Hall. *See* Mineral Industries Building

Hugo Black Room, 170

Hunter, Anna, 83

Ironic Classicism, 34, 35, 126, 131, 169

J. Nicholene Bishop Biological Station. *See* Tanglewood

J. W. Fiske and Company, 152

Jack (slave), 60, 61

James, Samuel, 60

James B. McMillan Building, 148, 155–56

James Knox Powers Hall, 117

Jasons, 60

Jefferson, Thomas, 4, 5, 17, 37, 128

Jefferson Hall, 43, 46, 60

Jemison, Robert, 14

"Joe, the," 178. *See also* Sewell-Thomas Baseball Stadium

John William Mallet Hall. *See* Mallet Hall

Johnson Barracks, 45, 53

Johnson, T. Earle, 119

Josiah Gorgas Hall, 168

Jones, Walter Bryan, 133, 190

Jones Hall, 117

Jordan, James Ralph "Shug," 156

Julia Tutwiler Hall (demolished). *See* Tutwiler Hall (demolished)

Julia Tutwiler Hall (residence). *See* Tutwiler Hall (residence)

Kappa Alpha, 24
Kay, Edgar B., 16, 189
Kennedy, John, 100
Kessler and Schillinger, 21
Kilgore, C. C., 83
Kilgore, Mrs. C. C., 83
Kilgore House, 78, 83–85
Kilgore Ranch, 83, 84
Kirkbride, Thomas Story, 151
Kirkbride Building, 148, 150–52, 157
Kirkbride Plan, 152
Knight, Eugene H., 24
Knight, William Paul, 177
KPS Group, Inc., 32, 125, 139, 171

Laboratory, 4, 5
Lakeside Dining Hall, 136, 145–46
Lakeside Residential Community, 136, 143, 144, 145
Law Center, 18, 28, 34, 46, 70, 74, 99, 166, 168, 170, 171, 187. *See also* Farrah Hall
Lawrence Whitten and Son, 146
Lee Barracks, 45, 53
Lewis, James Artemis, 25
Lewis Hall, 117
Lide, Martin J., 133
Little, William Gray, 86
Little Hall, 23, 26, 75, 78, 81, 86–87
Lloyd, Stewart J., 93
Lloyd Hall, 24, 27, 88, 92–93, 126
Lockwood, Frank, 20, 49, 66, 79, 80, 81, 85, 86
Long, Henry Sprott, 187
Lucy, Autherine, 99, 100
Lucy Clock Tower, 88, 99–100
Lupton Hall, 117
Lurleen Wallace Chapel, 156

Lyceum: University of Alabama, 4, 5, 9, 10, 19, 37, 40, 64, 67, 92, 103; University of Mississippi, 3
Lynchburg College, 10

Mabel Selden Byrd Hall, 108
Main Quadrangle. *See* Quadrangle, Main
Marian Gallaway Theater, 119
Mary Burke Hall, 26, 88, 100–101, 146–47
Mary Harmon Bryant Hall, 39, 41, 73, 120, 134–35
Martha Parham Hall, 26, 88, 100–101, 146–47
Maxwell Hall, 18, 36, 50–53, 58, 74, 95
McCauley, Charles, 95, 162
McCorvey, Netta Tutwiler, 81
McCorvey Hall. *See* Thomas Chalmers McCorvey Hall
McCowan, Edwin T., 25, 69, 118, 177. *See also* McCowan and Knight; Miller, Martin, Lewis and Edwin T. McCowan
McCowan and Knight, 25, 105, 141, 177
McDonald, Sidney, 167
McDonald Building, 166, 167
McLure, John Rankin, 113
McLure Library, 102, 113
McMillan, James B., 155
McMillan Building. *See* James B. McMillan Building
Madison Hall, 44, 45, 46, 60
Mal Moore Athletic Facility, 174, 177
Male Psychiatric Building, 154
Mallet Hall, 146
Malone, Vivian, 100
Malone-Hood Plaza, 88, 99–100
Manderson, Faye, 185
Manderson, Lewis M., 185
Manderson's Landing. *See* Park at Manderson's Landing
Manly, Basil, 18, 19, 40, 47, 48, 49, 60, 70
Manly Hall, 13, 62, 70, 71, 89, 98
Manufacturers' Association of Alabama, 81

Marion Military Institute, 11
Martha Parham Hall, 26, 88, 100–101, 146
Marr, William M., 1
Marr's Field, 1
Marr's Spring, 23, 36, 54–55, 76, 77
Marshall Space Flight Center, 124
Martin, Hugh, 25, 89
Mason, 37
Maxwell, Fred R., Jr., 52, 69
Maxwell Hall, 36, 51–52, 74
Memorial Coliseum, 176
memorial gate, 139. *See also* Crimson
    Promenade
memorial plaques, 41
Men's and Women's Tennis Stadium. *See*
    Roberta Alison Baumgardner Indoor Tennis
    Facility
Meridian Sash and Blind Company, 68
Miller, John Alexander, 25
Miller, Martin and Lewis, 25, 26, 35, 69, 86, 89,
    92, 93, 94, 99, 103, 105, 106, 107, 108, 110,
    113, 114, 117, 121, 122, 177, 182
Miller, Marin, Lewis, and Edwin T. McCowan,
    118, 123, 141, 177
Million Dollar Campaign, 20, 21
Million Dollar Plan, 20, 21, 22, 23, 24, 89, 103,
    118, 121
Mineral Industries Building, 27, 120, 123–24,
    129
Mitchell, J. T., 190
Modern, 34, 90, 95, 105, 118, 137, 142, 143,
    159, 162, 170, 181
Modern Classicism (Stern), 34
Modern Traditionalism, 35
Modernist, 34, 35, 95, 125, 126, 128, 139, 140,
    142, 146, 156, 169, 171
Montgomery, Jack, P., 93
Moody, Frank M., 169
Moody, Sarah, 72
Moody Gallery. *See* Sarah Moody Gallery
Moody Music Building. *See* Frank Moody
    Music Building

Moore, A. B., 86
Moore Athletic Facility. *See* Mal Moore
    Athletic Facility
Moore Hall, 26, 78, 86–87
Moral Treatment, 150, 151, 153
Morgan, John Tyler, 11, 80
Morgan Hall, 19, 46, 56, 69, 74, 78, 80–81, 98,
    111
Mortar Board, 43
Moseley, Carl M., Jr., 140
mound, 18, 36, 43–46
Moundville Archaeological Park, 189, 190–91
Murfee, James T., 10, 11, 12, 53, 58, 63, 64, 66
Murfee, John, 53
Music and Speech Building. *See* Rowand-
    Johnson Hall

Nash, Arthur Cleveland, 182
Nash, Richard, 190
Natatorium, 177–78
Nathaniel Thomas Lupton Hall. *See* Lupton
    Hall

National Oceanic and Atmospheric
    Administration (NOAA), 130. *See also*
    National Water Center Research Building
National Water Center Research Building, 120,
    130
Neil (slave), 58
Neo-Traditionalism, 35
New Hall, 23, 108
New York Wire Railing Company, 64
Nichols, William, 1–5, 17, 18, 20, 37, 43, 44,
    47, 55, 56, 58, 93, 186, 187, 188
Niles Bolton Associates, 142
NOAA. *See* National Oceanic and
    Atmospheric Administration; National
    Water Center Research Building
North Campus Recreation Center, 182
North Engineering Research Center, 120, 129
Northington Campus, 28
Northington General Army Hospital, 28, 142, 162

Nott, Josiah, 93
Nott Hall, 88, 93–94, 113
Nurses' Home, 24, 88, 96–97, 162

Observatory, 18, 36, 50–53, 58, 74, 95
Old Quad, 21, 25, 26, 27. *See also* Woods Quad
Old Quadrangle. *See* Old Quad
Oliver, John T., 74
Oliver-Barnard Hall, 13, 43, 45, 46, 50, 51, 62,
   72, 73, 74–75, 91, 92, 98, 142, 182
Olmstead Associates, 27
Ostling, E. J., 24
Our Students Our Future, 31–32, 185

Palladio, Andrea, 1, 35, 37
Palmer, Gordon, 135
Palmer Hall. *See* Thomas Waverly Palmer Hall
Palmer Lake, 136, 145–46
Pantheon, 37
Parham, Martha, 100
Parham Hall. *See* Martha Parham Hall
Park at Manderson's Landing, 16, 184–85
Parsons, Samuel, Jr., 14
Partlow State School, 140, 156
Patterson, John M., 133
Patterson, Sarah, 179
Patterson Champion's Plaza. *See* Sarah
   Patterson Champion's Plaza
Paty, Raymond Ross, 140, 155
Paty Hall, 136, 140–41
Paul W. Bryant Conference Center, 28, 29, 166,
   171–73, 175
Paul W. Bryant Hall, 117
Pearson, Tittle, Narrows and Associates, 137,
   170
Pennsylvania Hospital for the Insane, 151
Phi Gamma Delta, 24, 188
Phifer, Reese, 111
PH&J Architects, 116
Philomathic Literary Society, 45
Pickens, Israel, 2, 3, 4
Police Department, 166, 168–69

Porch, Ralph, 190
Post, George B., 20
Postmodern, 34, 35, 115, 126, 128, 131, 137,
   139, 157, 159, 161, 169, 182
Postwar Construction, 24
Powers Hall, 117
Pratt, Horace S., 60, 61
Pratt, John Wood, 57
Pratt, Mrs. Horace S. 61
Pratt House, 57
Presidential Dormitories, 23, 101, 117–18
Presidential Village Residential Community,
   136, 142, 144–45, 182
President's Mansion, 6, 7, 10, 18, 21, 23, 36,
   47–50, 56, 81, 86, 89, 93
Public Works Administration (PWA), 23–24,
   117, 121, 142, 154, 182
Pump House, 54, 62, 76–77

Quad. *See* Old Quad; Quadrangle, Main
Quadrangle, Main, 10, 21, 23, 27, 30, 47, 89,
   93, 105, 113, 117

Reese Phifer Hall, 25, 35, 102, 110–11, 137,
   162, 168
Reserve Officers' Training Corps (ROTC),
   47, 73, 74, 88, 91–92. *See also* Air Force
   Reserve Officers' Training Program; Army
   Reserve Officers' Training Program; ROTC
   Building
residential communities, 23, 30, 136, 142, 143,
   144, 145
Rhoads, Anne, 179
Rhoads, John, 179
Rhoads Stadium, 174, 179–81
Richard Channing Jones Hall. *See* Jones Hall
Ridgecrest, 23, 26, 30, 142, 145
Ridgecrest South Residential Community, 136,
   143
RISE. *See* Rural Infant Stimulation
   Environment
Riverside Residential Community, 136, 143

Roberta Alison Baumgardner Indoor Tennis Facility, 174, 179–8l
Roberts Brothers—Anderson and Co., Inc., 163
Robertson, R. H., 25
Rodgers, Eric, 130
Rodgers, Sarah, 130
Rodgers Library for Science and Engineering, 35, 120, 130–31
Roosevelt, Franklin, 89
Rose, Frank Anthony, 27, 105, 132, 141–42
Rose, Tommye Stuart, 141
Rose Administration Building, 102, 105–6, 114, 132, 138, 146
Rose Towers (demolished), 34, 136, 140, 141, 142, 145,
Rosser-International, 179
ROTC. See Reserve Officers' Training Corp
ROTC Building (Bureau of Mines), 88, 91–92
Rotunda: University of Alabama, 5, 6, 7, 8, 9, 18, 19, 21, 36–41, 44, 64, 89, 131; University of Virginia, 4, 5, 37
Rotunda Plaza, 41, 88, 89
Rowand, Wilbur, 119
Rowand-Johnson Hall, 24, 26, 27, 102, 118–19, 169
Rudolph, Jack, 60, 61
ruins, 8, 9, 10, 11, 21, 41, 44, 45, 46, 52, 63, 64, 67
Rural Infant Stimulation Environment (RISE), 158, 163
Russell, Julia, 95
Russell, Thomas D., 95
Russell Hall, 88, 95–96, 161, 162,

Sam Bailey Track and Field Stadium, 174, 177
Samuel Parsons and Company, 14, 18
Sarah Moody Gallery, 72
Sarah Patterson Champions Plaza, 174, 179
Save Woods Hall Campaign, 137
Science and Engineering Building, 120, 126, 127, 128, 129
Science and Engineering Complex, 126, 127, 128, 129, 162. See also Science and Engineering Building; South Engineering Research Center; North Engineering Research Center
seal: University of Alabama, 2, 3
Searcy, James T., 152
Sellers, James B., 41
Sesquicentennial Capital Campaign, 29
Sewell, Joe, 178
Sewell-Thomas Baseball Stadium, 174, 178–79
Shelby, Annette, 128
Shelby, Richard, 126
Shelby Hall, 31, 35, 120, 126–28, 154
Sherlock, Smith and Adams, Architects, 159, 161, 181
Shockly, Bascom T., 41
Shorter, John Gill, 53
Sigma Nu, 34
Sizemore, Raymond, 190
Skidmore, Owens, and Merrill, 171
Sloan, Samuel, 151
Smith, Eugene Allen, 8, 11, 44, 46, 51, 72, 81, 83, 94, 178, 190
Smith Hall, 19, 46, 72, 78, 79, 80, 81–83
Society of the Alumni, 14, 18, 20, 86, 172. See also University of Alabama Alumni Association
Somerville, Henderson M., 187
Somerville Hall. See Henderson M. Somerville Hall
Sorensen, Andrew A., 30, 126
South Engineering Research Center, 120, 128–29
Speake, Paul, 90, 109, 118, 119, 156
Speech and Hearing Center, 34, 158, 159–60
Springer, Mrs. E. C., 107
Stallings, Gene, 163
Stallings, Johnny, 163
Stallings, Ruth Anne, 163
Stallings Center, 158, 163

state architect: Alabama, 1, 3, 20; Mississippi, 3; North Carolina, 3

state engineer: of Alabama, 3; of Louisiana, 3

Stern, Robert A. M., 34, 35; *Modern Classicism,* 34

Steward's Hall, 5, 55, 56. *See also* Gorgas House

Stone, Edward Durrell, 170

Storr, Charles P., 41

Student Health Center, 158, 160–61

Student Recreation Center, 29, 174, 179, 181–82

Student Services Center, 136, 137, 138, 139–40

Student Union, 25, 110, 137, 162, 168. *See also* Reese Pfifer Hall

Summerour and Associates, Architects, Inc., 192

Superintendent's Mansion, 148, 152–53

Tanglewood, 184, 192–93

Temple Tutwiler Hall, 102, 109–10, 172

ten Hoor, Marten, 118

ten Hoor Hall, 27, 102, 118–19

Thomas, Frank, 178

Thomas, Joab L., 29

Thomas Chalmers McCorvey Hall, 146

Thomas Field, 26, 177, 178

Thomas Waverly Palmer Hall, 146

Thomas-Drew Practice Fields, 177

Tiffany Studios of New York, 41

Tiffany window, 41–42, 134

time capsule, 37

Title IX, 108, 109, 181

TMP Associates, Inc., 181

Touro–Shakespeare Almshouse, 12

Tram System, 32

Troughton and Simms, 52

Tudor Gothic Style, 8, 13, 63

Tuomey, Michael, 72, 74, 82

Tuomey Hall, 13, 43, 45, 62, 72–74, 91, 93, 142

TurnerBatson Architects, 95, 138, 161, 164, 168

Tuscaloosa County Courthouse, 1

Tuscaloosa Federal Building and Courthouse, 35

Tutwiler, Henry, 81, 192

Tutwiler, Julia Strudwick, 83, 85, 192

Tutwiler, Temple, 109

Tutwiler Hall (demolished), 78, 81, 85–86, 105, 107

Tutwiler Hall (residence), 34, 86, 136, 146–47

UDC. *See* United Daughters of the Confederacy

United Daughters of the Confederacy, (UDC), 41, 43

United States Department of Health, Education and Welfare, 135, 163

United States Forest Service, 105

Universitat. Alabam. Sigil., 2. *See also* seal: University of Alabama

University Club, 184, 186–87

University Medical Center, 158, 159–60

University Neighborhood Plan, 30

University of Alabama Alumni Association, 109, 110, 172, 173, 179. *See also* Society of the Alumni

University of Alabama School of Medicine, 93, 159

University of Alabama System Office, 29, 166, 167; former, 184, 187–88

University of Mississippi, 3, 5

University of North Carolina at Chapel Hill, 3, 4, 182

University of Virginia, 4, 5, 37

Urban Redevelopment Program, 26, 28

Urban Redevelopment Project, 27, 28

Vandegraaff, Adrian, 179

Van Keuren, Davis, and Company, 118

Vaux, Calvert, 14

Veterans' Emergency Housing Program, 24

Victorian Campus, 7–13, 62–77, 89, 170

Virginia Military Institute, 8–9, 10, 11, 12, 58
Volker, Joseph F., 188
Volkert, David, and Associates, 115
Von Braun, Werner, 124

W. B. Jones Hall. *See* Walter Bryan Jones Hall
Walk of Champions, 183
Wallace, George C., 100
Wallace, Lurleen, 156
Walter Bryan Jones Hall, 120, 133, 134
Ward, Jim, 163
Ward 34 West, 156
Warner, Elizabeth, 186, 188
Warner, H. D., 186, 188
Warner, Jack, 49, 186, 188
Warren, Knight, and Davis, 24, 25, 93, 108,
    111, 132, 154, 156
Warren, William T., 24
Warrior River. *See* Black Warrior River
Washington Hall, 43, 64
Watts, Thomas H., 53
Whilldin, D. G., 24, 95, 97
Whitten, Lawrence, 34, 100
Wickersham, J. B., 64
William (slave), 60, 61
William Stokes Wyman Hall. *See* William
    Stokes Wyman Hall
Williams Blackstock, Architects, 129, 190
Wilson Hall. *See* Augusta Evans Wilson Hall
Witt, Robert E., 31, 143
Women's Athletic Program, 108, 181
Women's Campus, 21, 26, 85, 86, 106, 108
Women's Reception Building, 25, 148, 154–55
Women's Soccer Stadium, 174, 179–180
Woods, Alva, 63, 168
Woods Hall, 11–13, 15, 34, 62–67, 70, 72, 76,
    89, 98, 103, 111, 113, 121, 137, 168
Woods Quad, 12. *See also* Old Quad
Woollen, Molzan and Partners, 169
Woolpert Consultants, 30, 179
Works Progress Administration (WPA), 145

World's Columbian Exposition, 16
WPA. *See* Works Progress Administration
WSV Architects, 143
Wyman, William Stokes, 83–84
Wyman Hall, 117
Wyatt vs. Stickney, 149–50

Yale Bowl, 182